WILLIE JOHNSON

PINNACLE OF PURPOSE

(Challenge to Excel)

From *Splinters of the Cross* Volume II New Edition

PINNACLE OF PURPOSE

(Challenge to Excel)

From *Splinters of the Cross* Volume II New Edition

WILLIE JOHNSON

ARPress
45 Dan Road Suite 15
Canton MA 02021
 Hotline: 1(888) 821-0229
 Fax: 1(508) 545-7580

Ordering Information:
Quantity sales. Special discounts are available on quantity purchases by corporations, associations, and others. For details, contact the publisher at the address above.

Printed in the United States of America.

 ISBN-13:   Softcover   979-8-89676-658-2
                      eBook   979-8-89676-659-9
                      Hardback   979-8-89676-660-5

Library of Congress Control Number: 2026902562

Pinnacle of Purpose
(Challenge to Excel)

This book is dedicated to millions of people around the world who have been redeemed by the blood of Jesus Christ the Lamb of God. Man's condition warranted God's intervention into history, to rescue us from eternal destruction.

This book is for those who get perplexed about the subject of suffering. My aim is to reveal through the scriptures that the favor of God creates pathways to victory in every dilemma in life; and that when we understand the reason behind our suffering it helps us to more freely access the help and support in scriptures that Jesus has made available to us. To be a Christian means to be a follower of Jesus the Christ. What He owns we own. Because He is blessed, we are blessed; blessed beyond measure for His great love with which He loved us.

The content of this book reminds us of our purpose, the reason why we are here; that reason being to share God's love with the world through the revelation of His Son who was the suffering servant. And to show to the world that suffering for Christ puts us to the advantage rather than a disadvantage. The backdrop of it all is with the expectation of drawing the sinner to Christ with a repentant heart. This book shows us that setbacks for Christ are actually set ups by God for everyone who will yield their lives to Jesus with total abandonment and without reservation.

Finally, this book is written to show that although no one enjoys suffering in any form, when we suffer for the cause of Christ, we discover the keys to being successful in our Christian life; a reality that most people it seems fail to realize. Life lived for the Lord Jesus will sometimes call for suffering of some kind, but the greatest thing about suffering for Him is that He never asks us to suffer without Him. He suffers through it with us, assuring our ultimate and triumphant victory!

Contents

All scriptures and scripture references are taken and quoted from the following Bible translations – King James (KJ), New King James (NKJ), American King James (AKJ), New International (NIV), and Complete Jewish Bible (CJB).

Acknowledgments

I would like to give a special thanks to the people that God has placed in my life who have helped me along the way in coming to where I am today, making this book available to public audiences.

Thanks to my wife Barbara; thank you for your help and support through many lessons well learned, in our personal lives and in the Ministry of The Gospel of Jesus Christ. Your love and care have helped in shaping me into who I am today. I also give a special thanks to the Congregation of Restoration Life Church Orlando for your prayers and faithfulness. Because of your faithfulness and your relentless support this book is made possible. Thanks to you all!

Contributing Editors

Editor one. . . . . Lord Song Publishing

Thank you, Lord Song Publishing, for your generous support in the editing of this book. Without your support it could not have come to its publishing stage. Thank you for a job well done.

Editor two. . . . . Barbara Johnson

Thank you, Barbara, for your faithful contribution to this book Pinnacle of Purpose and (Volume II of Where Godly Men Walked).

The time and hard work you have invested is priceless. Only the Lord Himself could reward you for your limitless sacrifice. I love you.

Editor Three . . . . Willie Johnson

My contribution is the joy of writing this book to the world to the glory of the Lord Jesus Christ.

Introducing
Pinnacle Of Purpose
(Challenge to Excel)

Suffering has been a major concern of mankind throughout the ages. It is as much a part of life as breathing, but no one enjoys it. If you or I had the option to choose between a life of pleasure and a life of suffering, the latter wouldn't stand a chance. Pleasure wins hands down, suffering is undesirable; it doesn't feel good.

This book is written not to mourn and groan about the woes of a life lived in a prison of suffering, but just the opposite. This book is born out of an appreciation for the life that is made better through suffering. It reveals to us the advantages and benefits of suffering for the cause of Christ. And that suffering for Jesus Christ is not to be viewed as a dreaded thing, but as a passport to the higher levels of service and grace awaiting us in Him; ultimately bringing us to Triumphant Victory.

My desire in writing this book is that as you read through its pages you will be able to see beyond the darkness that's often associated with our sufferings to viewing them as opportunities given to us by God to grow in Christ. As the Church and the body of Christ we are not exempt from suffering. In fact, in many cases we are actually called to it. Since there is no escaping the experience of it, we take courage and learn to embrace it as we begin the journey. By using every tool made available to us in God's Word we secure to ourselves this guarantee; that we are formed into the likeness of the Lord Jesus Christ.

So, join in with me in taking a different approach to suffering, as we view it from a different perspective. When we change our perspective, we will change our outlook. When we change our minds, we will change our lives.

"For I reckon that the sufferings of the present time are not worthy to be compared with the glory about to be revealed in us." Romans 8:18 (KJV)

Chapter 1

The Intervention of God

"In the beginning God created the heaven and the earth.

And the earth was without form, and void; and darkness was upon the face of the deep. And the Spirit of God moved upon the face of the waters.

And God said, Let there be light: and there was light..." Genesis 1:1-3 *(KJV)*

"God, who at sundry times and in divers manners spoke in time past unto the fathers by the prophets,

Hath in these last days spoken unto us by his Son, whom he hath appointed heir of all things, by whom also he made the worlds;

Who being the brightness of his glory, and the express image of his person, and upholding ns, sat down on the right hand of the Majesty on high: Hebrews 1:1-3 (KJV). all things by the word of his power, when he had by himself purged our sins, sat down on the right hand of the Majesty on high." Hebrews 1:1-3 (KJV).

The above scriptures describe God's intervention into a chaotic world of darkness to redeem His prize possession, Mankind.

Intervention:

The word Intervention comes to us here in the western part of the world from 15th Century Middle French or early Latin pronounced "intervenire". It means "to come between, interrupt," action taken to improve a situation.

Genesis one states: *In the beginning God created…* (verse 1) and…… The Spirit of The Lord moved upon (or hovered over) the waters… (verse 2b) It seems to describe a waiting period just before acting.

Chapter 3 of Genesis records that after our first parents Adam and Eve disobeyed The Lord committing the first sins of the human race in the Garden of Eden; that The Lord intervened. And after removing them from the Garden He pronounced upon them the consequences of their actions, and gave to them the Promise of *"The Seed of the Woman"* (Genesis 3:15). This was the first Prophetic foreshadowing of Jesus Christ, the coming Messiah and Savior of men.

Genesis 1:1 is clear as to what God has done in bringing creation into existence. *Genesis 1:2* seems to describe events which took place at another point in time, because it states that the earth was without form and void. Well, we know that our God is light, and there is no darkness in Him. In creating the light, His attributes and His nature declare to us that He is light.

Biblical Historians, Theologians and Scholars believe that between verses 1 and 2 of Genesis Chapter 1 is when Lucifer and the wicked Angels who decided to follow him in his campaign against God waged war in Heaven, and were cast out of Heaven into the earth.

After this, God announced that He would send a Savior in the form of a man to intervene on behalf of mankind.

Now that Satan is cast out of Heaven, he takes vengeance and carries out his wrath on the earth against mankind.

"Therefore rejoice ye heavens, and ye that dwell in them. Woe to the inhabitants of the earth and of the sea! for the devil is come down unto you,

having great wrath, because he knoweth that he hath but a short time."
Revelation 12:12 (KJV)

The wicked Angels were cast out from the presence of God.

Jewish history (The book of Enoch) has it that these rogue and disembodied spirits landed on earth in the Middle Eastern part of the world atop Mt Herman, which borders Lebanon and Syria. Jewish history also records that it was here where about 200 of them made this pact with one another to disrupt, corrupt, deceive, and to destroy mankind. So, they set out to implement their diabolical plan with the purpose of defiling the human race; expecting to prevent the coming of the promised *"Seed of the Woman"* (Genesis 3:15) from coming through the blood line of Adam. Right here is where Biblical history seems to agree with Genesis Chapter 6…

"Now it came to pass, when men began to multiply on the face of the earth, and daughters were born to them, that the sons of God saw the daughters of men, that they were beautiful and they took wives for themselves of all whom they chose." (Genesis 6:1–2)

They came into them and defiled them with hopes to prevent the coming of The Promised One, knowing that God would not send Him into the earth through a defiled body. Biblical Theologians and Historians believe that these Fallen Angels defiled the women by attempting to alter the DNA; causing the rise of a Hybrid Race. The offspring of this Hybrid race in the Hebrew language is known as the *"Nephilim"*. The name means the fallen ones. It is believed that these are the parents of what we now know as Demons presently in the world. These "Nephilim" were giants in stature (according to Genesis 6:4) went on to corrupt men and women, and on to defile even the birds and beast. Could this explain the reason that all around the world excavators are digging up the remains of Dinosaurs which are literally being found in the most remote Nations of the world?

The Bible records that God Almighty intervened on behalf of mankind by dispatching Michael the Arch-Angel and a host of His faithful Angels against these trespassers (The wicked Angels) and set the time for their destruction. God passed sentence upon them and banished them into places of darkness. The worst of these, those who left their first estate (according to The Book of Jude 1:6) and defiled the Women, are now bound under chains of darkness in a place in the underworld called "Tartarus" in the Greek language, which is a place of punishment. Some of the other wicked Angels were thrown into what the Bible calls *"The bottomless pit"* (The Abyss) which also is a place of punishment. Read *Revelation 9:1-12*.

According to Revelation 9:14, Four of them are awaiting their judgment on *The day of The Lord*, are bound and held fast under the great Euphrates River which runs from Southern Turkey north of Israel, to the country of Kuait south East of Israel.

Satan is allowed to remain loose for a season where he temporarily acts as the *"Prince of the power of the air" (Ephesians 2:2)*. That means that he influences many of the ideas which come through Government system in our present world. According to the Word of the Lord in Revelation 20:2, during the Millennial (Thousand year) Reign of Christ, Satan will be cast into the Abyss/bottomless pit and kept confined there until he is loosed for his last season to ever trouble mankind again.

But the point I want to make is that behind it all God is in control of times, dispensations, seasons, and everything that pertains to mankind.

When God's people are in any trouble, He sets the day for their deliverance; and no one can ever cancel out His plans for them.

It will all come to pass according to God's timing; and on His schedule nothing happens too late.

When God first began His deliverance of the Nation of Israel, He began to manifest it through Abraham; and through the years it passed on to his descendants just as The Lord had promised.

Israel's deliverance from Egypt was not a hap hazard sporadic or happen by chance event; no, it was planned out and timed out by God to happen when it did, where it happened and how it happened.

God also had a set time for the entrance of Jesus His Son to come into the world.

Isaiah 9:1-2 says — "But there will be no gloom for her who was in anguish. In the former time he brought into contempt the land of Zebulun and the land of Naphtali, but in the latter time he has made glorious the way of the sea, the land beyond the Jordan, Galilee of the nations.

The people who walked in darkness have seen a great light; those who dwelt in a land of deep darkness, on them has the light shone." (ESV)

The prophecy is true! In our days we can rejoice because the *"Seed of the woman"*, The promised One, The Messiah, Jesus Christ has come, and He has promised to work His will in our lives. For that reason, we can take courage and live for Christ.

Jesus intervened for all of humanity while in the Garden of Gethsemane in intercessory prayer. Because of His great sacrifice on the Cross at Calvary, we have been set free to serve Him. He has given us a purpose, and He has secured our destiny. Now let the Journey begin!

Progression and Accuracy of God's Word
(The Origin of Man)

"This is the book of the generations of Adam. In the day that God created man, in the likeness of God made he him;

Male and female created he them; and blessed them, and called their name Adam, in the day when they were created." Genesis 5:1-2 (KJV)

My aim in this section is to remind you of the trust worthiness and accuracy of God's Word.

Chapter five of the book of Genesis gives us a detailed description of the origins of mankind. It records the Genealogies of the pre-deluge Patriarchs; showing to us how God started the human race.

In reading the book we are reminded that God's Word is immutable (unchanging) and that He will always accomplish what His determines.

The following scriptures speak of God's Immutability, read - *Psalm 118:89; Numbers 23:19; and James 1:17.*

The overlapping years for the first ten generations from Adam to Noah, we know them because they are recorded. But no one can establish the date of creation. Beginning with the time of Abraham Theologians can begin with more accuracy to calculate years.

Genesis 5 – Adam's family record

Let's take a brief look at Adam's family record; in so doing we will see the awesome for-knowledge of God, and the accuracy of His Word.

In early Biblical times, the Hebrews (also known in later times as the Jews) gave their children names which were of great significance. We will explore the significance of Adam and the names of his descendants.

<u>Adam</u> - Adam's name means "From the ground, or from the clay, *Red*". The Bible pictures Adam as the crown of God's creation. He was created in the likeness of God to live in fellowship and to fill God's desire for him by implementing His will in the earth. This was and still is God's determination. Millennia's have passed, people have changed, and many things around us have changed; but God's purpose for mankind has not. Although Adam and Eve committed high treason in the Garden of Eden, God still works out His original plan for mankind.

<u>Seth</u> – Seth's name means Appointed. According to Genesis chapter 5 verse 3, Seth was born when Adam was 130 years old; … *"a son in his likeness and image"*. Biblical history has it that Seth was born after Cain murdered Abel. His genealogy is repeated also in *1 Chronicles 1:1–3. Genesis 5:4–5* states that Adam fathered *"sons and daughters"* before his death aged at 930 years. Seth lived to the age of 912.

<u>Enos</u> – Enos is the son of Seth. His name means Mortal. At this time humanity was truly experiencing the effect of mortality (The state of being subject to death).

<u>Cainan</u> – Cainan, son of Enos; His name means sorrow. In the Garden of Eden because of Adam's disobedience everyone born after him would experience the effects of physical and spiritual death. Ever since death was introduced to man it has always brought sorrow with it.

<u>Mahalalel</u> – His name means "The blessed God". Regardless to man's sins, our God was and is and will always be the blessed God who is ahead of it all. He holds the future in His power.

<u>Jared</u> – Jared's name means, "Shall come down". Wow, now that's a name to remember. How would you like to have a son with that name?

Next there is <u>Enoch</u>. His name means Teaching. Although all the Patriarchs are to be revered, Enoch plays a very special role in Biblical history. The Bible says that *"he walked with God, and God took him ..."* *Genesis 5:24 (KJV)*. This means he did not die a physical death (See also *Hebrews 11:5) He is the seve*nth of the ten pre-flood <u>Patriarchs</u>. I see Enoch being the seventh generation from Adam as God's perfection or number of completion. God was now making changes for the Generations to come.

Compare the accounts of each of the other pre-Flood Patriarchs who lived above seven hundred years. Enoch lived for 365 years, a much shorter life span. Although a shorter life span, the favor of his success was that he *"walked with God"*. ...*Then men began to call on God...* *(Genesis 4:26c)*

The taking away of Enoch also reminds us of the coming event of the rapture of the Church spoken of in *I Thessalonians 4:17*, Read it.

<u>Methuselah</u> - His name means "His death shall bring". The meaning of his name may have seemed a bit unusual to his peers, but it would be significant in God's strategic plan for the future of mankind.

<u>Lamech</u> - The name Lamech means "The despairing". His name is a reminder of life conditions in his day.

<u>Noah</u> - The meaning of Noah's name surely was a sigh of relief and hope to his people. His name means Comfort, Rest.

He is the only Patriarch that is known as the pre and post flood Patriarch. Noah is representative of the transition from the old to the new, from darkness to light; from a world perishing to salvation.

Adam	-	Man
Seth	-	Appointed
Enos	-	Mortal
Cainan	-	Sorrow
Mahalalel	-	The Blessed God
Jared	-	Shall come down
Enoch	-	Teaching
Methuselah	-	His death shall bring
Lamech	-	The despairing
Noah	-	Comfort, rest

Unlike the order of the previous Patriarch's genealogies; at the outset of this verse, it emphasizes… *"and **begat a son:"** (Genesis 5:28).* Noah would be the son that God would use for the salvation of humanity. Compare Noah's position, with that of the coming of Jesus Christ God's (only begotten) Son for the salvation of mankind.

So, what is the reason for it all concerning these Patriarchs, and what is the story behind the meanings of their names?

Well, just as the footprint of a man leaves an imprint or shape uniquely to him; and as a fingerprint specifically identifies an individual, here in the meanings of these names we can see the undeniable hand work of God. Let's take a look at what we have.

It reads - <u>Man</u> <u>appointed</u> <u>mortal</u> <u>sorrow</u>, (but) <u>The blessed God</u> <u>shall</u> <u>come down</u> <u>teaching</u>. <u>His death shall bring</u> <u>the despairing</u> <u>comfort</u>, (and) <u>rest</u>.

How Awesome is that? God's methods may not always be according to what we understand, but they always accomplish what He has set out to do. In this life many times we are met with sorrow, and we find ourselves desperately seeking a way out. But God always brings us comfort, because He is... *"the God of all comfort"* according to *II Corinthian 1:3-5 (KJV)*. So, the journey goes on.

Today we are faced with the same struggles of life as they did in the beginning. Jesus brings us comfort as we read the Holy Scriptures.

But we must keep up our guard in those times when we have been comforted. We must not allow ourselves to get too comfortable, because when we do, there is a danger of becoming complacent, which encourages us in getting used to where we are. But the Christian life is not designed for us to plateau. It is designed for us for us to continually progress to greater levels of maturity in Christ.

From personal experience, many times when the Lord is ready for new growth to take place in my walk with Him, I find myself feeling satisfied where I am; not wanting to get out of my comfortable place.

Now there is at Jerusalem by the sheep market a pool, which is called in the Hebrew tongue Bethesda, having five porches.

In these lay a great multitude of impotent folk, of blind, halt, withered, waiting for the moving of the water.

And a certain man was there, which had an infirmity thirty and eight years.

When Jesus saw him lie, and knew that he had been now a long time in that case, He saith unto him, Wilt thou be made whole?

The impotent man answered him, "Sir, I have no man, when the water is troubled, to put me into the pool: but while I am coming, another steppeth down before me."

Jesus saith unto him, Rise, take up thy bed, and walk. John 5:2-3; 5-8 (KJV)

Escape From Your Comfort Zone

Our bed is what we lie upon each night. It is an instrument that is designed for sleep, comfort, ease and rest. It is a good thing to have in your possession. Some people sleep on their sides; others are more comfortable lying on their back. Some people are even able to rest lying on their stomach. Whatever suits you best, if it works sleep!

But when it comes to spiritual things the place of resting in a comfortable position just may not be the best place to be in. Of course, this man lying by the pool was not just resting on his bed, but he was in a position that he needed to get out of. This man's dilemma speaks to us about how we can stay in the place where we are for too long. Sometimes we need to be shaken out of our comfort. Jesus was about to rock this man's world. Jesus would finally bring this man out of the place that he was used to; and into the place where he so desperately needed to be in.

Our comfort zone is the place that we are used to, the place where we put forth the least effort. It's the place where we feel safe from whatever may be required of us.

Our comfortable place in our Christian walk can be the place where we so easily put off praying until tomorrow, or when there is a need, we say I don't feel like it today, there are others who can do it, let them do it.

Can you imagine waiting for something for 38 years?

I'm not saying that this man was comfortable lying by the pool for thirty-eight years, but he no doubt may have gotten used to being there. What do you think, and what do you see when you read the scripture concerning this man's dilemma? Some have suggested that he should have found a way to get into the pool within the 38 years. Others say he was just too slow, and some say he didn't want it bad enough; and so many other reasons are given. At the very least, he had perseverance. But Jesus didn't dwell at all on the reason he was there for so long. He was more concerned about making the man whole.

Consider this: while in certain seasons of life waiting is the appropriate thing to do, perseverance in any season is always the thing to do.

Whether this man had gotten comfortable or just use to being in that position we don't know, but we do know that he needed to be delivered. He needed something (in this case) someone to shake up his world.

Regardless of his reason for being there for so long, he had the recipe for his breakthrough within himself. He had at least three things that were working in his favor.

(1) He believed he could be healed.

(2) He was expecting to be healed.

(3) He put no limit on time.

Apparently, he was not intimidated by the length of time which had passed because he kept on trying to get into the pool.

And now his breakthrough was at hand. Although he was looking for it to come in one way, it was about to happen in a totally different and unexpected way; God had a better way for him.

When Jesus asked him do you want to be healed, it was not that Jesus didn't know if he did; it was to ignite the man's faith to believe for what Jesus was about to do.

Without hesitation the man responds - I want to, but I'm not physically quick enough to get into the pool before someone else gets in first (Paraphrase). He's really saying I can't do this with my own strength.

Have you ever been there at the place of *"I can't do this in my own strength?"* We all have been there, and for some of us; multiple times in life.

Yet we can read throughout the scriptures and see where Jesus shows up to shake up the normal flow of things in people's lives to get them out their comfort zone, that is, out of their own way and into God's more excellent way.

"…But covet earnestly the best gifts: and yet shew I unto you a more excellent way." 1 Corinthians 12:31 (AKJV)

Many times, we spend our lives trying to figure out things that the Lord has already set up to happen in its time. The key element to receiving our petition is our consistency while waiting for Him. Our victories are not won in a comfort zone, but in a battle zone.

Leisure is apt to produce complacency, while a battle brings us victory.

Ecclesiastes 5:3a tells us - *"For a dream cometh through the multitude of business."* It indicates that the dream is realized while one is busy; and in our case, busy doing the will of God.

Consistently living in expectation of the Lord's intervention on our behalf will bring us out of our comfort zone. As we allow Him, He brings us to unknown before experiences in Christ; and to greater levels of service for Him. His presence with us brings us to realizing our purpose in life, and to our potential and worth before Him. These could never be realized or accessed if most of our life is spent living in a comfort zone.

Chapter 2

A Life with Purpose

"In the beginning was the Word, and the Word was with God, and the Word was God. He was in the beginning with God. All things were made by Him, and without Him was not anything made that was made." John 1:1-3 (NKJ)

Many of us learned this scripture along with other children sitting in our Sunday school classrooms, while others perhaps in familiar surroundings at home with family. Each time I read this verse I think of our heavenly Fathers' authority. For me it adds a feeling of security, which speaks of God's Omnipotence (absolute power). We read of God's awesome power first of all in creation in the book of Genesis *"In the beginning God created the heavens and the earth." (1:1)*

He is Alpha and Omega, (the first and last). The evidence of His presence is seen in all of creations by people of all nations.

"The heavens declare the glory of God..." Psalm 19:1. Verse 3 of the same chapter says, "There is no speech nor language, where their voice is not heard."

Speech and language speak of people, cultures and Nations. The Bible is filled with stories of different ethnic groups of people who accepted God's plans for their lives; and in the process were led to realizing their purpose in life. Through challenges and changes thousands and even millions of them were delivered from seemingly impossible situations.

With some of these we can identify, because we have the same experiences. As we read through the pages of the Bible, we can find one example after another of the victories and defeats of men and women who chose either to trust God and then were blessed, or who failed to trust Him and were not blessed. This is a theme which runs throughout the entire Bible. Mankind has been given the power to choose, but our choices are not always the right one.

But despite men's wrong choices, God is in control. That is why He gave us His Word, the Holy Bible. The Bible is a book of Divine laws and instructions which provide the knowledge and understanding sufficient for mankind to live at his highest potential before his creator. Because is it a book of divinely orchestrated events, ultimately it is designed to reveal to us the redemptive work of Christ, which is man's salvation. This salvation brings to us God's grace. Through faith in Jesus His Son we are brought to the knowledge of our God given purpose. Jesus came to earth with a purpose; to restore mankind through a relationship with Him. Through that relationship man realizes his purpose.

Along with the awesome plan of bringing men to their purpose Jesus would be tempted, tested, tried and then finally put to death on a cross. This was the price He paid for our salvation. On the way to realizing our purpose, our faith will also be tested.

"Beloved, think it not strange concerning the fiery trial which is to try you as though some strange thing happened unto you." 1 Peter 4:12 (KJV)

Remembering that our Lord bore a cross gives us great comfort and strengthens our faith. We need to have strong faith, faith that endures. Strong faith is faith that has been tested. We find our purpose in Him when we allow Him to strengthen that faith.

"But without faith it is impossible to please Him…" Hebrews 11:6a (KJV)

While our faith is being tested and we are realizing our God-given purpose, it is good to be mindful of this truth; that the Bible is not as much about our faith being on trial as it is about God's love being on trial. I will speak more about His love in a later chapter.

When God spoke His creation into its existence, He had a purpose in mind for all of mankind, which started when God gave to Adam his instructions on taking proper care of the Garden of Eden. As it was with Adam, so it is today. The Lord still expects men and women everywhere to obey his voice and live according to His Word, with the expectation that His ways may be known, and His will be done on earth as it is in Heaven.

The Bible never indicates to us that Adam physically saw God, but it simply states that God talked with him.

This gives us a mental picture of faith at work. Learning to trust in a God we cannot see is faith. After the fall of man in the Garden the real test of his faith began. God would allow the testing of Adam's faith to continue, passing on to succeeding generations. Attached to it were the purposes of God for all of humanity.

As it was with Adam, so it must be with us, that our faith will also be tested. Habakkuk 2:4b says: *"For the Just shall live by faith."*

In order to get the very best out of a life of faith, one must learn to live a faith-filled life. And the only way to do that is to be led by the author of faith; The Holy Spirit.

"For as many as are led by the Spirit of God, they are the children of God," *(Roman 8:14). Also, he tells in Galatians 5:16, "This I say, walk in the Spirit, and you shall not fulfill the lusts of the flesh."*

When we walk in the Spirit we have liberty; but if we walk after the flesh, we leave ourselves open to attacks from Satan which gives him a place in our lives and enables him to take back spiritual territory that Jesus our Savior has won for us.

"Walking" in the above verse doesn't mean just physically walking, but it speaks of a lifestyle or manner of living. Anyone walking (living) according to the flesh has no protection against the attacks of the enemy. People who live according to the flesh create a platform upon which the enemy can launch his arrows of deception upon them. This is where Satan has deceived many into thinking that having faith in God's doesn't work.

But on the contrary; having faith in God does work! We were created to live by faith and to have continual fellowship with God through Jesus the Christ of God and Savior of sinners. His plan of salvation reveals the depth of His love for us, proven through the giving of abundant life here on earth, and the promise of eternal fellowship with him forever. So, we stay on guard with our faith shield up.

"Be alert, be sober minded, because your enemy the Devil prowls around as a roaring lion looking for someone to devour."(I Peter 5:8)

In my lifetime I have seen too many Christians fall away and became deceived because of their choices to live by the standards of the flesh. That doesn't work. It only forces one's life into a downward spiral. It is a place out of which only The Holy Spirit can deliver them. The Bible calls it carnality when people live according to the desires of the flesh. They fall into a carnal lifestyle and go on like nothing is wrong. This is also infectious, because their casual attitude about their sin will eventually cause others to stumble. Anyone who lives that way will always lead others astray. We cannot allow ourselves to be deceived because our God is Holy. Carnal thinking will never receive God's endorsement; neither can self-willed men win His favor.

They need only to repent and remember God's Word which says…

"Because it is written, be ye Holy for I am Holy." (I Peter 1:16)

When men are willing and obedient in turning to God with a sincere and repentant heart, God abundantly pardons, forgiving every sin. God's determination is to fulfill all of the promises He has made to those who love and keep His commandments. He has a purpose for every man woman boy and girl, and He will work His will in the one who is willing to put their trust in Him.

"If you are willing and obedient, you shall eat the good of the land." Isaiah 1:19

Have you ever wondered how a Holy God can call people who are sinners by nature, His own? The answer is that mankind was in the hand of Almighty God before he fell under the corrupt and Satanic rule which presently governs much of the world system.

God redeems men and women, saving them from the corruption of sin and from Satan the great deceiver, who would rob them of their God given privilege to live victorious lives in the Lord Jesus Christ. The Bible lets us know that we were without God in the world and alienated from the life of God and the covenant of His promise of the salvation which the Lord Jesus Christ now brings. We know that this wonderful salvation is founded upon God's Word. It was not instituted when Jesus came to die on the cross, but it was established before time itself began.

"According as He has chosen us in Him before the foundation of the world, that we should be holy and without blame before Him in love: Having predestinated us unto the adoption of children by Jesus Christ to Himself, according to the good pleasure of His will.

...To the praise of the glory of His grace, wherein He hath made us accepted in the beloved." Ephesians 1:4-6 (NKJ)

The Lord settled the issue of salvation first, and then Jesus came to rescue us. When we receive Him as our Savior, we come into covenant with him. And in order for us to receive the benefits of that covenant made with us through Jesus Christ our Savior, we must become faithfully committed to His word. When we surrender our will to Him, we are put in the position to receive God's best, which results in a life with purpose.

Divine Appointments

God's desire has always been to bless his people. That being said, we must realize that we have been divinely appointed to a life of faith.

"Now the Lord had said to Abram: Get out of your country, from your family and from your father's house, to a land that I will show you. I will make you a great nation; I will bless you and make your name great; and you shall be a blessing. I will bless those who bless you, and I will curse him who curses you; and in you all the families of the earth shall be blessed." Genesis 12:1-3 (NKJ)

God was not just making a suggestion when He told Abram to come out from his family to go into the land he and his descendants would inherit. It was a command with a promise, and a Divine appointment with God that must be kept.

Everything in God's creation has a divine appointment attached to it. Simply put, everybody and everything must respond to God's command and purpose for them according to *Ecclesiastes Chapter 3.*

The sun has an appointment ordained by God. Daily it rises in the east and completes its circuit setting in the west. The stars never appear at high noon. They are appointed to the night seasons only. Observe the moon. Although you can see it in the daytime hours at times, its appointment to glow is at nightfall so that men can see at night. We don't experience sub-zero weather in the middle of summer in the United States. That's because the seasons have been appointed by God to happen as they do. The diversity of God's creation speaks of His knowledge and divine authority. Not a single element in His creation has the option to keep silent; all must respond to him. The existence of God alone demands from his creation a cry of "worthy are you oh Lord, all creation is filled with your glory!"

Although evil is rampant in our world today, God is and always will be in control. It is only a matter of time when He will set everything in order and bring it all to a close; and making His enemies His Foot stool as He promised in His word.

Jesus' mission in coming to earth was a divine appointment. He came into a world corrupted by sin so that you and I would come to know our Heavenly father's love for us. *Isaiah 63:1-6* tells us, *"He speaks in righteousness, is mighty to save, and He treaded the winepress alone"* *(paraphrase).*

This means that no one else was sufficient. No one else has the power to forgive our sins; nor conquer death Hell and the grave. He and He alone is the Savior, He knows all about us, who and where we are, our financial status, our emotional and spiritual state. His coming affected everything that pertains to the human race.

His appointment was to rescue us from death and destruction to a life of righteousness, peace and joy in the Holy Ghost. Jesus' love for us is so great that He willingly suffered the pain of death on a cross for people who did not deserve it, in order to purchase our salvation. This great salvation brought us abundant life on earth and eternal life with Jesus when life here on earth is no more.

After Jesus ascended to His father, He fulfilled his promise sending to us The Holy Spirit, the comforter who guides us into all truth. Only the Spirit of truth can lead men into the truth. As a part of His role toward humanity, the Holy Spirit daily seeks to bring us to new heights of maturity in Christ Jesus.

The men who crucified the Lord Jesus thought they were in control, but they were not. Although they carried it out, His death on the cross was not accidental, nor was it co-incidental; it had been planned beforehand. It was a Divine Appointment.

Death on a cross was seen by society as punishment for the worst of sinners. Jesus bore this degradation of the cross like punishment for a sinner. But though bearing the shame of the cross, He would arise in the glory of the king. And by this glory He brings many sons to glory. Cross bearing always comes before the glory can be revealed. Overcoming the resistance of our flesh is cross bearing. No doubt, this is one of the greatest opposing forces to our victory, because our flesh never wants to experience pain of any kind.

Jesus was fully God yet fully man. He experienced every man's struggle in human flesh before and on the cross. But He could not allow the discomforts of His flesh to be a cause to abort His mission. This is a good lesson for us to learn. An eternal reward is always greater than momentary suffering.

From the earliest stages of Jesus' earthly ministry people tried to set up roadblocks in His path to get Him off course. They tried to set traps attempting to catch Him in a lie. He was faced with different kinds of opposition. Support for his earthly ministry first of all should have come from the religious leaders of His day, but instead this was where he faced great opposition. Yet He still showed them His love! The Prophet Isaiah and others had foretold of Jesus suffering and rejection. His humility is an example for us to mimic.

"Though He were a Son, yet learned he obedience by the things that He suffered." (Hebrews 5:8-14)

In every part of Jesus' earthly life, we can find something to apply to our own which teaches us that we have been divinely appointed to share his word with others. Names and titles mean very little to God, for there is no big I nor little you with Him; but simply servants. Whether we are well known or not so well known, we all are destined for a divine appointment with God.

"That at the name of Jesus every knee should bow, of those in heaven, and of those on earth, and of those under the earth, and that every tongue should confess that Jesus Christ is Lord to the glory of God the father." Philippians 2:10-11 (NKJ)

The above scripture describes the ultimate and final appointment that each of us must prepare for while we are here on earth.

An appointment is a scheduled meeting between parties. As you know sometimes when we make appointments, circumstances may call for a change of plans, or even a cancellation altogether.

Even in serving the Lord with the best of intentions from a heart of sincerity we will have challenges which cause us to make new arrangements from our original plans in order to reach a goal or accomplish a task. But there will be no cancellations with our God as far as finishing the course of life. We are called to an appointment with a destiny that cannot be revoked. We are called to be like Jesus; we are called to bear a cross as he did.

Jesus' sacrifice on the cross shows us two things. First of all, it shows us His great power to save us. And second, it shows us the extent of our need for a Savior, which is what the cross is all about. We place ourselves in His most intense gaze and draw His attention when we take seriously what He did for us on the Cross. It is time to take a closer look at the Cross. Then after careful observance, we must take it up (as Jesus did) and carry it, because we have an appointment with destiny. God created the seed that would grow to be the tree that men would cut down to shape into the Cross upon which His Son would be hanged.

Ephesians 1:20 tells us - "Jesus has been raised up and is now seated at the right hand of the father in the heavenly places."

Jesus was destined for the cross; which also meant ultimately He was destined for the glorious victory that would follow. He bore His cross for us over two thousand years ago. We may never have to literally be nailed to a cross in order to get the victory and experience the joy of overcoming like Jesus did, but we must bear the cross of test and trial while we are being transformed into the people he wants us to be.

II Timothy 2:11-12 tells us, "This is a faithful saying: For if we be dead with Him, we shall also live with Him: If we suffer, we shall also reign with Him."

Before we can enjoy the final victory Jesus intended for us, we must accept this truth; that along with the joys of the Christian experience, the cross of Christ is not so crumbled that there is none of it left. There remain splinters of the cross of Christ, with some leftover nails for each of us.

Mentors, Mentors, Where are the Mentors?

"But now is Christ risen from the dead, and become the first fruits of them that slept." I Corinthians 15:20 (KJV)

The words "first fruits" in the above verse means first partaker, or leading example. One who is the first partaker or leading example of something is a mentor. Jesus is our perfect example of a mentor; He is Righteousness personified. He is the greatest mentor of all.

The one who leads by example is able to have a positive influence on others leaving a legacy to them. We need more men and women who are mentors for good.

I am saddened over the decline of mentors for good. What is worse is that this has happened among our Christian brothers and sisters over the past twenty years. There needs to be more of an impartation of

Christian values into the next generation. As in a relay race, we must pass the Baton to them so that they may carry it on to the finish line.

Yet even after a decline in mentors, I can see the hand of God uncovering a new breed of men and women that He has prepared for the end times. I believe somewhere in the shuffle we lost the definition of what a real mentor is. We all like the idea of being a leader with a title attached to our name, and having others to look up to and admire us. But having a title attached to our name and being able to gather followers is no guarantee of affective mentoring. Judas who betrayed our Lord fits that narrative. He was named one of the master's disciples, but he pretended to be a faithful follower of Jesus. Soon deception was his undoing. Being called a disciple alone was of no benefit to him without a true heart commitment to what was right. Had he chosen to do so, he could have been a faithful follower of Jesus just like the other disciples. They learned faithfulness through their experiences with Jesus. Experience may be the greatest asset a mentor can possess. The most affective things a mentor shares are usually from their own life experience. In a word, you must live it before you can give it. A mentor is one who is able to lead others by example through experience. Jesus led by example, and whatever He shared with others was always something he had experienced. He only said and did what his Father communicated to him.

A mentor is a leader; and the one who would be the greatest example to others is the one who has learned to be a good follower. He or she knows that instruction and discipline are keys to successful mentoring.

"Though he were a Son, yet he learned obedience, by the things which he suffered;" Hebrews 5:8 (KJV)

Godly mentors are made through adversity. This is where discipline and godly characters are developed. Adversity is a word that most of us would like to erase from our vocabulary. But the truth is, God uses adversity in developing mentors for his kingdom.

Have you ever wondered why God allows you to go through some things? He always has a reason for it. It's called character development. Have you ever found yourself at a job where you and your employer's personalities were like two sheets of sandpaper rubbing against each other? Or what about the driver of the other car on the roadway on the day you are running behind schedule? He pulls out in front of you; causing you to slam on the brakes to avoid a crash… "Wow that was close," only to watch him go one block and turn onto a side street. These may seem to have little or nothing to do with the character development of a mentor, but actually they play a major role in it. In this kind of situation God is looking at the attitude of our heart toward others. He wants us to yield our will over to His will. When this happens, our first response to other people when differences arise; will be to ask ourselves what would Jesus do? When we respond to them in the right way, the first thing they will notice is a good attitude which makes them open and receptive to the love of God being expressed through our lives. God can use us as mentors for others. He requires only a willing and obedient heart.

Sometimes others can see the mentor qualities in you.

It is an honor to be chosen by the Lord to mentor others. That means He trusts you to draw them to Him.

But not everyone is excited when they see God using you. Strangely some people out of jealousy and even have stood in the way of potential mentors for Christ. The fearful refuse to rise up in obedience and go forward. Instead, they hesitate, they whine and they grumble which empowers their fears to keep them spiritually stagnant. This is complacency. It ignores the call of the Holy Spirit who is calling us to a higher level of grace and revelation by the power of God.

Mentors need vision, because vision brings change, and change is inevitable to life. Some people will only live for themselves, following their own ways and traditions and not willing to change. Whenever people refuse to change, they are strangled by their own life pursuits, then they become frustrated and offended at God when life doesn't turn out the way they expected it to. We need to be open to the leading of the Holy Spirit; and accessible to Him because the next generation needs mentors like you and me.

"Where there is no vision, the people perish: but he that keepeth the law, happy is he." Proverbs 29:18 (KJV)

Change is a cross that a mentor for Christ must bear. Everyone who would be a mentor for Christ will experience the ongoing struggle between the flesh (which leads us out of the way) and the Spirit (who leads into the right way).

Jesus experienced this conflict of the flesh and the Spirit.

When Judas and the soldiers came upon Him in the garden of Gethsemane, Jesus had just experienced what is known as "the great struggle" (war between the flesh and the spirit). Our flesh tries to dominate our spirit. But as we obey God's word and live in the Spirit, we don't walk after the carnal ways of the flesh. Thus, by robbing the flesh of it power we are over comers for the cause of Christ.

The on-looking world then sees in us God's idea of a real mentor.

Good mentors are not found only in the church, but that is where the world expects the most affective ones to come from. My prayer is that the Lord will give us spiritual sight to recognize the work of the Holy Spirit as He seeks to produce godly mentors in our generation. When men and women are open to His leading, we are sure to become mentors to others.

An affective mentor is one whom the trials of life have reveal to them their own weaknesses, and yet refuse to retreat. They also recognize that mentoring others for Christ often puts them in at risk situations, but they know that their lives will impact others for good for generations to come. The next generation will benefit from your experience as the man or woman who is a mentor for Christ.

Now, have you ever seriously asked yourself this question, whose lives have I affected for good for the Savior?

It may not always be easy becoming the kind of mentor God wants you and I to be, because most of the time that calls for the stretching of our faith. But by putting our complete trust in Him, we become candidates for Divine experiences. It is a process, and we must learn to trust the process. Only then will we realize how our lives can impact others for Jesus. If you are a wise mentor, you will surround yourself with people wiser than yourself.

"Where there is no counsel, the people fall; But in the multitude of counselors there is safety." Proverbs 11:14 (NKJ)

Chapter 3

Greatness by Design

*"For the eyes of the Lord **run to and fro throughout the whole** earth, to show Himself strong on behalf of those whose heart is loyal to Him...." II Chronicles 6:9a (KJV)*

God still speaks to people who will take the time to listen. He desires to share His heart with each of us as He draws us to Himself.

The watchful eye of our Lord beholds the sons of men throughout the whole earth. From the wealthy to the poor, from the college professor to the uneducated; without discrimination God seeks men. Their status doesn't matter, because He is looking at the priceless treasure of potential which He has placed within each of us. For millennia God has specialized in developing His character within His people. He is able to bring great things out of a life completely yielded to Him. What does greatness look like through His eyes? The greatness I'm speaking of will not stamp on your Chest MMOG, (mighty man of God), or MWOG (mighty woman of God). The truth is, greatness is by God's design, and it can only come through God's process. God wants to reveal to the world His greatness through your life and mine. He doesn't look for a ready made subject. Instead, He looks for someone who will trust His strength and His development process. Though frail as we are, He works through us, despite our weaknesses; and makes what seems impossible possible. He does this as we yield to the leading of the Holy Spirit. The Holy Spirit enables men to do the will of God. As we place our lives in

His care, trusting and daily seeking Him, He accomplishes great things in and through us.

Unlike the world's idea of greatness, their focus being more on accomplishments and the accumulation of things; this greatness is not something we seek after, it is the treasure of God's favor; something we inherit the moment we receive salvation.

"Not by works of righteousness which we have done, but according to his mercy he saved us, by the washing of regeneration, and renewing of the Holy Ghost; which he shade on us abundantly through Jesus Christ our savior, that being justified by his grace, we should be made heirs according to the hope of eternal life." Titus 3:5-7 (KJV)

Personally, I think it is greatness to simply wear the name of Jesus. Understanding that we are not justified by anything that we can do frees us to trust and depend on Him and not live life by default. Living by what Jesus has already done is living by design.

To be "great" according to Webster's collegiate dictionary, (notes 3 and 11) it means, "remarkable in magnitude, degree, or effectiveness, used as a generalized term of approval".

When we think of someone great, usually we picture someone who has been successful at something. The truth is, people have differing definitions of what greatness is, and they achieve it in different ways. There is the world's definition of greatness; but then there is God's definition of it. The world labels its success (i. e. financial status or excelling on the corporate ladder etc.) as forms of Greatness; and certainly, there is nothing wrong with great accomplishments, and being successful. But success in God's eyes is when men are led straight to the heart of God. When we have made it a lifestyle of sharing His love with others, which is what Jesus has done for each one of us. It is the process of transforming the lives of men and women, and connecting them to the heart of their Heavenly Father. Jesus is in the business of raising men and women to greatness. Greatness as men know it focuses mainly on the present. But by God's design; the greatness He seeks to bring out of our lives serve a twofold purpose. First, (for the present) God brings men to greatness so that others can realize that the earth and its resources belong to Him, and that He is able to take care of His own.

"The earth is the Lord's, and the fullness thereof; the world, and they that dwell therein." Psalm 24:1 (KJV)

Second, (for the future) Jesus' power to transform men and women from sinners into "sons" of God leads succeeding generations to set their hope in God as he prepares them for eternity.

"Who shall ascend into the hill of the Lord? Or, who shall stand in His holy place? He that hath clean hands and a pure heart; who hath not lifted up his soul unto vanity, nor sworn deceitfully. He shall receive the blessing from the Lord, and righteous from the God of his salvation." Psalm 24:3-4 (KJV)

God has been transforming the lives of ordinary people into men and women of greatness for thousands of years. Everyone He raises, He orders their steps in His word. By His design He strengthens them through character development. This process sometimes includes ridicule rejection, and even some injustice by other people. But these are key elements in character development. The Old Testament book of Judges gives us an example of this truth with a man by the name of "Jephthah". *In chapter 11:1-3, we can see Jephthah* suffering injustice at the Hands of his brothers. But God would take his rejection and turn it around for good. Verse eleven of the same chapter lets us know that when the threat of war arose in Israel, the same people who had rejected Jephthah now needed his military abilities. The people made him a captain over the armies of Israel.

Our Lord Jesus, just like Jephthah; experienced rejection by his own people; so He understands our grief when we endure such things. Jesus can relate and sympathize with us when we suffer in life situations.

"For we have not an high priest which cannot be touched with the feeling of our infirmities; but was in all points tempted like as we are, yet without sin." Hebrews 4:15 (KJV)

The scriptures show us that not all of the Jewish Leaders would accept Jesus as the Messiah. Most of the Pharisees took Jesus to be just an ordinary man. They did not believe that He was truly the Son of God. The only thing they took seriously about him was the threat his message brought to their pious ways of life. But their negative responses could not cancel the Lord's Great plan of salvation brought to men. This great salvation would come just as promised. Jesus' transition from suffering servant, to Glorious and Victorious King would be known by the whole world.

God would allow His son to be scoffed at, ridiculed, Mocked and beaten, treated like a condemned sinner, and finally put to death. But that was the purpose behind it all. Death was no match for the greatness emerging. Jesus was God in the flesh, He was and is already great, but He must complete this process and become the first fruit of the resurrection. He could see the final victory beyond the cross that lay Him, but He must first endure the Cross. The thing which His flesh did not want to experience, (the cross) would be the instrument used in obtaining the victory. As the flesh dies the spirit brings life.

Now you may be experiencing a flesh killing trial right now; you know that area of your life where there are hidden faults that the Spirit of God exposes to you so that you can yield them to him for correction. This is where we bare our cross; but also, where we.... *"Cast all our care upon him, because he cares for us." I Peter 5:7 (KJV)*

Jesus wants the on looking world to see our response to suffering. They need to see our faith in action.

Sometimes we fail to respond properly to the Holy Spirit's promptings. Our flesh may want to draw back sometimes from the way in which God chooses to show his great strength through our weakness. But faithfully reading God's Word keeps us fully prepared so that at any given moment we can be faithful witnesses for Him in our daily life.

Keys and Crosses

Everyone who lives for Christ bears a Cross. Our cross is like the key which fits only a certain lock. Our Cross (tests, trials, temptations, storms, and other experiences of life) which we bear for the sake of Christ is extended to us in measures, in exact measure enough to attain our victory. In a word, it is shaped to your and my specificity like a key made to the specs of a lock. If you can receive it, your Cross is the connection and the link attached to your victory; it is victory by design. God in His wisdom has calibrated our challenges, our bruises, and struggles; and in the process He has tempered us (made us ready) for this our present season.

Keys are cut to fit certain locks. They are instruments we use which allow us to enter and exit spaces. Keys have a two-fold purpose, to lock, and to unlock. A key is not made to open all kinds of locks (Although you can make multiple keys for one lock) they all are made to fit the specs of that one. You have heard the expressions "The key to it all," or "He holds the key" or "such and such is the key factor". These things speak of the main element that is the driving force behind it all. Our faith and trust in The Lord are the driving force behind it all to lead the way. It is the key which unlocks doors into our victories that lie ahead of us. Learning to hear and apply God's Word will unlock doors of blessing. Our sensitivity to grasp what He is saying to us in this hour will also lock out the unwanted and the things that would harm us.

Over the span of your life and mine, it has been a process of shaping, and cutting, prodding and contouring, to prepare us for what is before us right now. It has been designed by God that the challenges now facing us have come to open the next chapter of our lives. As children of God, we all have a cross to bear. Whether we experience rejection or some other kind of hardship; when we endure, God always brings us to blessing as we continue to serve Him faithfully. Jesus' passion in being our sacrifice for sin was that salvation for men would raise them to sons of Glory (Greatness). And even after the cross, Jesus still intercedes for us to our Heavenly Father as the process of fitting us into His plan and shaping us more into His likeness continues. He holds the keys that unlock the potential which He has placed within each of us. And through His great sacrifice, victory is attainable by way of the cross which He bore for each of us.

After Jesus' resurrection, everyone who saw and heard the news could not deny the power and glory that was now revealed. He is a Great God who does great things, and who brings greatness out of those who put their trust in Him. A life designed and shaped by the hand of the master; this is true greatness!

Iron Sharpens Iron

You have heard the expression *"Iron Sharpens Iron"*. This statement describes two elements or materials of the same caliber, density or abrasion; when scrubbed together they produce some benefit for both. This expression can be used to describe how the Lord sometimes uses life situations for our spiritual growth. He may use a scenario where people with different personalities and opinions end up in the same place as an opportunity to broaden their sense of comprehension. Overcoming differences is a major task for some people. Jesus' earthly ministry brought Him into places where He faced people who had different views and opinions, even about who He was. His aim, regardless of their disposition, was always to look beyond the exterior and to keep His focus on what mattered most. He sought for ways to connect with them by sharing the love of God with them. He has a way of bringing good things out of bad situations, allowing the good to outshine the bad.

Challenging situations for a Christian can be seen as splinters of the cross that Jesus bore for us. These are good examples for us which will enable us to overcome differences when it comes to responding to others who may not share our passion. Everyone has their own opinions, preferences, and ideas. There is no man or woman on earth who agrees one hundred percent with others, but that's the uniqueness of how the Lord has designed each of us. One good thing about life is that people learn to adjust. We can agree to disagree. Whatever situation life may bring, the key is to let the expression of God's love be paramount.

From the cradle to the grave Jesus experienced every part of life that we could imagine. And this was His one aim and whole purpose, to share the love of God with others. Knowing that the cross was before Him would not make Him take a detour. On the contrary, His love for humanity would cause Him to forge ahead for our redemption. From the first crack of the Roman soldier's whip to Jesus' last breath on the cross He carried the weight of the world, the sins of mankind upon Himself. His flesh was literally crushed, but He did it all because of His love of mankind.

It doesn't seem likely that many Christians if any in our present day will be hung on a cross literally for our faith, but we can be sure that in different ways we will experience the Savior's cross.

His cross was not destroyed that there are no splinters remaining. And for sure there are some leftover nails for every Christian experience. But don't lose heart at the thought of suffering for Christ. *I Timothy 2:12 tells us… "if we suffer with Him we will also reign with Him."* Because of His plans for us we have this promise, when it's all over, thanks to Him *we win!*

The problem of suffering has been a great concern of mankind for thousands of years. Sometimes it comes in a not so intense way. At other times suffering shows up like an abrasive scrub against our lives. But we must not forget that suffering for Christ brings us to our highest good in life. When we suffer for Christ, we are being fitted for eternity. Any way we look at it we are blessed when we remain faithful to Him. He is transforming our mortal bodies into glorified bodies while our service to Him is bringing glory to His name.

Glory! The road to glory is a rocky one that few people travel because it will cost us our life, literally a life of sacrifice.

In Old Testament times, the every day order of service for the Hebrews was to offer the sacrifice of one type of animal or another depending on what the occasion called for. The death of the sacrifice was required to be accepted on an altar to atone for the one who brought it. This system operated upon the terms of a covenant that God had established between Himself and the children of Israel.

We live in the New Testament age, the age of grace. And now Jesus is looking for living sacrifices, people who are willing to trust Him to empower them for victorious Christian living, which begins here on earth and is realized in its fullness when we receive our reward in heaven. This is made possible through the covenant He makes with us through His blood which was shed on the cross.

Under the Old Testament Covenant with Israel, if the people followed God's precise instructions, they could rest assured that God would be faithful to His word in doing what he had promised. Their sacrifices were of sheep and goats and heifers.

Jesus Christ is the same yesterday, today and forever. Jesus invites everyone to be a part of this New Covenant which also is ratified by blood. But this blood is not that of animals. It is the pure and sinless blood of the Holy Lamb, the only begotten Son of God. Everyone who will receive him as Lord and Savior has His promise of eternal life.

In chapter twelve of the book of Romans, the apostle Paul compelled the Christians to *"present your bodies a living sacrifice holy and acceptable to God."* Unfortunately, the biggest problem with the living sacrifice is that it (we) keeps crawling off of the altar whenever we have to suffer for Christ. Most people don't like to suffer or face difficulties; because it means we are asked to come out of our comfort zone.

Jesus wants His children to learn to lean on Him at all times, and especially when things don't go well. We are called to serve the Lord with gladness, even in times of crisis, and not with dread, or complaints. In the difficult times is when God shows us his abundant grace.

Once I heard a story of a man who was worrying about his problems, so he decided to go for a walk. The more he thought and worried about them the worse he felt about his life. So, he began to complain. Suddenly he heard the most beautiful and melodious song being chirped by a bird somewhere in the bushes just off the road he was traveling. The sound was so sweet to the ear that it interrupted his focus on worry. And off the road he went going to see what kind of bird it was. After waning his way through the brushes and stepping into a clearing, he observed a most eye-opening combination. The beautiful song he had been listening to came from a wounded bird whose leg was caught in a branch of the ground brush. While being amazed at the sight of that combination, God spoke to him and said, see, I can bring beautiful things out of the worst situations.

Does your cross seem too heavy today? If that bird, though being wounded can bring forth the beauty God intended for it, what does this say to you and me? Out of all God's creation we are especially loved by him, so we can always trust him. We must learn not to be surprised when we find ourselves in difficult situations, tests, or trials. Jesus our savior already told us to expect these things to come, and to ... *"count it all joy"* when we do, according to James 1:2 (KJV).

So, if you have buckled or fallen down under the pressure of your dilemma, by His strength you can bare up under the weight of it; it will soon be over. Reclaim your witness and your testimony and keep on standing, because you have been called to blessings through these with the promise of a reward afterward. Satan your adversary wants to destroy your testimony, but you wear the name that is above every name, the name of Jesus. When your testimony for Jesus is under attack that's when God is in the process of making it stronger.

"Now Peter sat without in the palace: and a damsel came unto him, saying, thou also was with Jesus of Galilee. But he denied before them all, saying I know not what thou sayest." Matthew 26:69-70 (KJV)

Earlier in verse thirty-three of the above chapter, Peter had declared, *although all men shall be offended because of thee, yet will I never be offended. But n*ow Peter was being attacked for the testimony which he held. Yet Jesus had already prayed for him that his faith would not fail. Jesus already knew that it would not fail, but Peter had yet to realize the strength of it through an attack on it. This trial of Peter's faith would strengthen his commitment to Christ later on, and these brazen attacks would sharpen his testimony to be more effective. If our testimony and our witness for Christ is never attacked, we will never know if it is effective. The integrity and strength that godly men and women possess is born out of the testing of their commitment to Him.

When we read the scriptures, we realize that God has so much for His children to enjoy, and He will not fail to bring us into it. But to allow all this without conditioning us by test and trial first would prove to be tragic for us. My experience has been that nothing just happens by divine osmosis. God has a plan that although it may call for suffering now and then along the way, this is the tool He uses to rub out all that He cannot use in our lives. The brazen trial is what strengthens us and makes us vessels of honor for His use. It is a process that He has used for thousands of years in shaping the lives of His people. His way for us has always been to progress through a process like "Iron sharpens Iron".

The Test of the Heart

"Moses my servant is dead; now therefore arise, go over this Jordan, thou, and all this people, unto the land which I do give them, even to the children of Israel." Joshua 1:2 (KJV)

The children of Israel had finally come to the border of the promise land. These were the descendants of the original families that had come out of Egypt. God had protected them in their wilderness journey, as He would remind them later.

"And I have led you forty years in the wilderness: your clothes are not waxen old upon you, and thy shoe is not waxen old upon thy foot." Deuteronomy 29:5 (NKJV)

The Israelites wilderness experience had been a forty-year trial of their faith to determine whether they would learn to obey their God with a true commitment from the heart. They were now about to begin a new chapter in their lives, which would reveal where their heart really was as they entered into the land they had long waited for. But even here they would be faced with new challenges to test their faith and their commitment to the Lord.

What happens with you after you have received what you have prayed for and waited for from the Lord? Does it motivate and energize you to go higher, or do you become relaxed and satisfied?

The Israelite nation could not afford to relax now that their prayers were being answered, and neither can we. In fact, this was the time for them to ramp up their prayers, become more faithful, and to be more thankful to God for this mighty deliverance to them. It had been a forty-year heart commitment development campaign. The strength of one's true heart commitment is developed over time.

*"And now, Israel, what doth the Lord **thy God require of thee, but to fear the** Lord **thy God, to walk in all his ways, and to love him, and to serve the** Lord **thy God with all thy heart and with all thy soul,** To keep the commandments of the LORD, and his statutes, which I command thee this day for thy good?" Deuteronomy 10:12-13 (KJV)*

Israel was called to a life of faith. As with Israel, so we have been called to a life of faith in Christ, with the expectation that through life's changing seasons our commitment to Christ grows stronger. But that commitment cannot be made strong without some testing along the way. Now no one ever gives a test with the intention of failing you, but it is to prove you so that you can make the necessary adjustments. The testing of the hearts of God's people in the wilderness prepared them for their victories in the promise land.

People often use the expression "experience is the best teacher". If that is true, then surely after forty years of wilderness wandering the people of Israel should have been scholars at living victoriously.

After forty years some of them may have thought now the testing was finally over. But the truth is, passing one test brings us to the place that demands more experience. That same heart commitment to Jehovah in the wilderness would be required of them for their victories in the new land.

What about your faith; and what is your heart committed to? The Greatest test that you and I face may not be the dust we're breathing in a hot desert experience of our lives, nor the difficulties we endure when faced with a wilderness experience. The greatest test of our heart commitment toward God will probably be in our promise land; right over there by the pomegranate, where we are tempted to relax and forget that the rest of the world exists.

This story of God dealing with His people in the wilderness is about much more than correcting them for the error of their ways. The wilderness had been a place of preparation for Israel, which draws for us a vivid picture of the Lord strengthening his people's relationship with him, and preparing them for greater responsibilities for what lay ahead of them. Jesus wants you and I to be a relational and responsible people.

It was crucial for them to be relational. Relational because The Lord their God wanted to have a close relationship with them. And responsible because they were not poor people, they had wealth in the wilderness. With wealth comes responsibility. Their fathers had brought with them the wealth of Egypt when they began their journey. Unlike the treasure used in rebellion with the golden calf, the faithful among the Israelites used their treasures from Egypt mostly trading among themselves.

Although they had gold, silver; and other precious metals, God wanted them to remember that He was their source. This is why they did not suffer hunger, because He had supplied all their needs. And now the question was, after praying and waiting for so long; would this new generation be willing to put their wealth to the use of establishing and implementing God's works in a new land where they would no more be mobile? They could not afford to yield to the temptation of being careless and forgetful saying no more trouble, we have finally arrived. Just as Israel needed to take this warning seriously, we too must be wise and learn from our past mistakes so that the experience we have attained won't be wasted. As the Lord takes us from one level of maturity to the next, He expects us to grow in the knowledge of Him and walk in His wisdom.

The people of Israel had learned in the wilderness that experience gave them the upper hand in some situations, while in others they had faced defeat without it. Now they were ready to enter into new territory with new challenges which would test their heart commitment to Jehovah. After all their experiences, the question remained, where was their allegiance, and to what or who was their heart committed to? Was it in their abilities, did they still walk in fear, or had they finally learned to completely trust in God? They would need to be confident with unshakable faith upon occupying the new land that God had given to them. God was promoting them to a higher place of service for Him.

"For promotion comes not from the east, nor from the west, nor from the south. But God is the Judge: He puts down one and sets up another." Psalm 75:6-7 (KJV)

The Lord delights in bringing us to new heights and into new places of service for Him. New places of service may not necessarily require prior experience, but promotion never comes without it. The Lord always prepares us in advance before bringing us into the place of blessing. Experience gives us knowledge, Knowledge brings with it understanding; and with understanding only can wisdom be applied.

Usually, people who are promoted are they which have experience. When the experience of one's life is on a continual upward swing, they are living life with momentum. The whole purpose behind experience is that we are growing to new levels of maturity in Christ. Maturity is not an option if we would be successful in what we do for Christ on this Christian journey.

Unlike their forefathers, this generation of the Israelites would be serious about their service to Jehovah. The wilderness had put them to the ultimate test of their faith. It had given them time to search their own hearts resulting in a greater appreciation for God's care of them.

Our faith is made strong when it is tested. As Jesus builds up His Church we are in transition through the testing of our faith. A strong Church is what God uses to put down the forces and powers of darkness. God can use a congregation of believers whose hearts are fully committed to the Lordship of Jesus Christ. Through our faith and by His power, He can change the hearts of the people of the world so that His righteousness might fill the whole earth.

"For the earth shall be filled with the knowledge of the glory of the Lord, as the waters cover the sea." Habakkuk 2:14 (KJV)

On September 11, 2001, the United States suffered terrorist attacks on New York City, Washington D.C. and Pennsylvania. A short time later, the people of Afghanistan felt the heat of retaliation for harboring the terrorists. President George W. Bush Jr. sent U.S. armed forces, with Allied nations to wage war on the people of Afghanistan at a level that was referred to as "A new kind of War". The President's strategy was of such that he persuaded nations around the world to get involved in the fight to wipe out terrorism. It was a move that created a global net, which left the terrorists literally with few places in the entire civilized world to hide. The idea was that if the United States could make a big enough splash that the rest of the world would feel the waves and spring into action against terrorism. It took a different kind of strategy to overpower a different kind of enemy. The body of Christ can learn much from his strategy.

Evil men were behind it all and they are to be blamed for those terrible crimes and attacks against humanity. America along with other nations must take this as a wakeup call, because as a people and a nation we have turned away from God in our hearts. He has given His abundant grace to us for centuries and commanded us to teach His ways to our children; as well as reaching out to other Nations and blessing other people.

Moral decay has been eating at the core of our nation for a long time now. We must not press upon God's patience. May God have mercy upon us and help us not to forget His works, that His Word is true, and that we are in his hand.

Evil minded men have been trying to undermine the operation of God in the United States for decades now. They are twisted and subtle in their thinking, even after the workings of demonic and Satanic forces to overthrow our nation. We must be strategic in waging Spiritual warfare in this hour. The first step to assure our victory over them is to recognize that we have left our first love and repent before our God. The Apostle Paul declared to Timothy that he must… *"war a good warfare"*.

For us that means, not only to fight, but to be wise and strategic in how we fight.

In this 21 Century Church we may use some different strategies than in those days, but our weapons remain the same....

"For the weapons of our warfare are not carnal, but mighty through God to the pulling down of strongholds;" II Corinthians 10:4 (NKJV)

So, it is clear that the Lord is looking at the heart of mankind to see if He can trust us to be responsible with what He has delegated to us. We must be completely convinced that our God will do all that He said in giving us the victory. Although we are faced with wars on the land, our ultimate warfare is not physical but spiritual. It is the battle of good versus evil. When we apply God's word to our everyday life we overcome and experience victories that Jesus has already won ahead of us.

Proverbs 13:22 tells us that "the wealth of the sinner is laid up for the just."

The Lord will take the wealth from the wicked (those who are spoiling society, robbing the poor for gain, and abusing the resources of the earth) and transfer it into the hands of His people for the building up of His kingdom on earth. But this transfer won't be without some challenges; challenges to our trustworthiness, honesty and our commitment to remain faithful to God after He has brought us prosperity. The temptation to accumulate stuff and things is near the top of the enemy's list of distractions, which focuses more on our agenda, than God's agenda.

And He said unto them, Take heed, and beware of covetousness: for a man's life consisteth not in the abundance of the things which he possesseth." Luke 12:15 (KJV)

The above verse is not suggesting that God doesn't want us to have some things, but the opposite. He doesn't want things to have us. He is the source of life who gives us the power to get wealth and to prosper. We must always remember that there is no resource without the source. Jesus is our source.

Throughout biblical history we can see continued battles, then victory, battles, then victory. Victory never comes without a battle because victory is never just handed over, it has to be won. This is what Jesus did on Calvary's cross for you and I when He won the ultimate victory. This victory provides everything you and I may need that pertains to life and godliness. Remember that it's so easy to lose our focus through the changing seasons of life, and to set our hearts on our accomplishments and enjoyment of life experiences. The question remains as the daily events of life tugs at the motive within us asking that haunting question, where is your heart? We must never forget what God has done for mankind through the coming of Jesus Christ our Lord. He has blessed us beyond measure. With such Divine favor on us, we must wake up each day, and look into the mirror, ask the one looking back at us this question. Is my life all about the blessings, or is it about He who does the Blessing?

*"For the eyes of the Lord **run to and fro throughout the whole earth, to shew himself strong** in the behalf of them whose heart is perfect toward him." II Chronicles 16:9b (KJV)*

The nation of Israel was now about to enter into the greatest season of their lives, and everything hinged on their heart commitment to the Lord their God. The condition of one's heart will determine the quality of their dwelling place.

The Lord always brings deliverance and gives us victory by testing the will of the heart. When we allow His testing to be complete, His Kingdom advances in our lives.

*"The humble shall see this, and **be glad: and your heart shall live that seek God.** " Psalm 69:32 (KJV)*

Chapter 4

The Process

The Bible speaks to us of many heroes of the faith, and we admire them for such great faith. We have a tendency to capsulate the whole story of their lives in the few words "Great faith". But the reality of this is that their faith didn't become great overnight. God brought them to that faith through a Process. Everything happened in *Due time. Due time is the fulfilling of time which has been set for a particular event. It agrees with an appointed time.*

Throughout the span of time, we can see that God's dealings with mankind is never accomplished without a process. Faith building is a process. Everyone experiences a process of some kind now and then, but it is the ones designed by God that count the most. Jesus took about eighteen years (from ages 12 to 30) to prepare for His Ministry, and three years preparing His Disciples as they traveled from place to place. His whole mission was about the process of preparing His Disciples to change the world by impacting it with the Gospel. God's process always rolls out His plan right on time.

As we observe Abraham, we can see God's timely process in action as he was commanded to sacrifice his own son Isaac on an altar. It wasn't a voluntary decision on the part of Abraham; it was God's plan, God's timing, and all God's doing. He chose Abraham, He chose Isaac also for the sacrifice; but the center of focus in the story was as much about the development (the process) of Abraham's faith, as it was about the man himself.

"And it came to pass after these things, that God did tempt Abraham, and said unto him, Abraham: and he said, Behold, here I am." Genesis 22:1 (KJV)

The scripture says, *"And after these things,"* after what things? If we will look back to Genesis 21:14 we can see that God had begun the process of fulfilling his promise to Abraham and Sarah. But they became impatient along the way. Impatience will always get us into trouble. Waiting is a virtue. Waiting has a way of bringing out the best and the worst in people. People who don't have good motives won't wait long because they're not interested in the commitment it takes to see something through. They're too interested in short-term gains or success. Patiently waiting on the Lord builds anticipation and transforms our character as well as intimacy and dependence upon God. The good news is that The Lord never asks us to wait without Him. Waiting during the difficult times developed Abraham and Sarah's relationships with God. The reason we get to read the stories of these great men and women is because they learned to successfully go through the difficulties of their lives. They experienced the process with God and then at the end they enjoyed the promises of God.

Did you know that God is just as interested in the journey as He is in getting us to our destination?

Abraham and Sarah needed to learn that waiting on the Lord Builds Patience in their Lives. The first thing That God would do was to make some adjustments in the weak and flawed areas of their lives through challenges that would strengthen their faith for the promises ahead.

This event pertaining to Isaac took place after the conflict about Ishmael had been resolved. Ishmael had been born to Abraham by Hagar Sarah's maid. There arose anger and resentment between the two women because of the birth of Ishmael. The book of Galatians compares this natural situation to the spiritual and calls it an Allegory, or we would say a metaphor to describe the significance of the two.

"Nevertheless what saith the scripture? Cast out the bondwoman and her son: for the son of the bondwoman shall not be heir with the son of the freewoman." Galatians 4:30

Through Hagar Ishmael is compared to what is accomplished through the ways of the flesh, while Sarah and Isaac are compared to what happens through God's promise.

There will always be conflict where there are two opposites in the same house. Hagar is referred to as the bondwoman, because Ishmael's birth was a result of the will of the flesh. But Isaac was born to Abraham's wife Sarah; having been promised by God was a reference to freedom. There is always a conflict between the flesh and the spirit, it is impossible to walk in the spirit while living according to the ways of the flesh; the one will always cancel out the effects of the other.

Casting out the bond woman (the sinful ways of the flesh) and living according to the will of God enables us to grow through this process and strengthens our relationship with Christ. Then are we sons and daughter of the free woman (recipients of His promises).

Before we came to Christ, Satan held us in darkness where we could not receive the promises of God. But Jesus brought us salvation and forgiveness which has set us free. As we yield to the process, we can experience the abundant life that Jesus purchased for us to enjoy here on earth, and eternal life with Him in Heaven.

We are victorious in Him as we work together with him.

"For we are laborers together with God: ye are God's husbandry, ye are God's building." I Corinthians 3:9 (KJV)

Through His awesome faith developing process, the Lord brings forth the people He Has uniquely fashioned, revealing to the world His matchless design!

Was Jesus a Politician?

"My people are destroyed for lack of knowledge: because thou hast rejected knowledge, I will also reject thee...." Hosea 4:6 (KJV)

In this section I want to focus on spiritual and political situations. In some cases what is said may seem contradictory to some Christian's world views in matters of church and state.

Now before you view these as two entities that cannot co-exist or feel the need to arise and defend your Christianity against political matters; please allow me this luxury to speak about them.

I know that you have heard people make the statement... *"being so heavenly minded yet of no earthly good"*. It simply describes one fantasizing about going to a glorious place (Heaven) while ignoring the demands and needs (of earth) that are presently around them.

My desire is that after you finish reading this book you will have a better understanding of your place in time and history, and that you will be reminded of our responsibility as Christians and citizens of our nation and to be prayerful. But also, to become actively involved in this fight against the evil that threatens our well-being as believers and as a Christian nation. Knowledge is power!

I want to show you in simple terms and everyday language that what you don't know could harm you.

"Let every soul be subject unto the higher powers. For there is no power but of God: the powers that be are ordained of God." Romans 13:1 (KJV)

Scriptures that speak to us about people in political situations are spread throughout the Bible, some of them are directly focused on, while others indirectly. God often brings His people into places of influence where they can have a public voice.

The man Daniel served in the Palace at Shushan according to *Daniel 1:19-21*. Some years later Nehemiah served as the cup bearer to the King *(Chapter 1:1)*.

Then there was Joseph whom God raised up and placed him the second person of authority in the kingdom to Pharaoh King of Egypt *(Genesis 41:37-41)*.

Need I mention Queen Ester with the favor of God bestowed on her? Then there was New Testament Saul of Tarsus. Before his conversion he was part of the political party known as the Sanhedrin. And the Bible speaks of many others who were active in government affairs, influencing their generations for God from a political position.

The theme which runs throughout the scriptures is projected in the words "The Savior of sinners". This is why Jesus came into the world, to save sinners, and that encompasses the whole man as well as the wholeness of mankind, the spiritual and physical part of man. God is our creator and He reserves the right to fill every part of our lives with Himself.

The Lord has always wanted His people to be in places of influence whether in or out of political environments where they can affect good changes in the world. He led our forefathers who founded this great Nation of The United States of America to establish it upon Godley principles. They were religious men and women who treasured living by their Godley values.

Now we have the "Separation of Church and State". Over the centuries this narrative has pushed out our God-given privilege and religious freedoms. I personally believe that a Nation that was founded upon Godley principals declaring to keep Godley standards should not depart from them. Looking at the condition of people's lives in our Nation today it is apparent that we got off track somewhere along the way. And now for the last sixty years or so religion has been restricted to guidelines controlled by the Government.

"Blessed is the nation whose God is the LORD, the people he chose for his inheritance." Psalm 33:12 (KJV)

Who created the Church, and who established the state or government? It doesn't take a rocket scientist to figure that one out. God is the Lord over them both. Many of us may not be politically savvy, but that doesn't mean that we are not to be involved in politics. The Pledge of allegiance to our Nation's flag declares that we are "One nation under God". We must pray for our Nation, for our President and all of our officials in Washington DC who enforce our laws and set policies for the Nation, because their actions directly affect you and me. The times in which we live warrant our undivided attention on these matters. My observation has been that many in the Christian community don't seem to care much about political matters. It is a fine line that is separating what is permissible between matters of Church and state. As Christians and citizens of a country whose foundation rests upon our Godly values and right morals, it is crucial that we never forget where we came from. It is not only a privilege that we can get involved with whatever promotes rightness and fairness, but it is also our God-given responsibility to do so. We must get beyond feeling that it's a disservice to Christianity when we speak or act on certain political issues. Without sounding Judgmental, it seems that for decades the Church has been lulled to sleep on matters of what we can or cannot do when it comes to being patriotic and what our privileges are as citizens. We have acted as if we can just pray and look the other way and somehow the atrocities of corrupt individuals in our government will just go away. But no, on the contrary; you and I must get busy. You say busy how? I'm glad you asked!

First of all, we are part of God's family, children of the eternal King. Second, we are citizens of this nation with certain inalienable rights according to our Constitution. That means you and I have been provided with certain privileges intertwined with the laws of this land to enjoy. But some of us have not even taken the time to discover them. We have been given the right to practice our religion (although Christianity is not just a religion but a relationship with Jesus Christ) we have the privilege to vote for whomever we choose. We are free to take part in whatever supports wholesome values, and which promotes what is right. Also, we can have a voice in what takes place in our Nation. At the risk of being called a fanatic misled by error, I would like to share my heart with you on these urgent matters. My hope is to awaken you to the reality that as Christians the abundant life that Jesus purchased for us is not just a spiritual blessing that will come in the sweet by and by as some often portray it. But it includes the real here and the now. God has blessed us tremendously as a nation like no other nation for centuries. But our freedom is under attack, and we can't afford to sit idle and do nothing about it.

In present day America we have been under attack by those who hate our way of life, one among many is Islam. You have heard of Sharia law. It is the law under Middle Eastern Islam which governs a way of life that stifles civilizations and chokes out establishments with a false religion. It is a known fact that it is a threat to every Christian and the victory that Jesus Christ purchased for you and me.

The Bible says there is no other name whereby men can be saved than by the name of Jesus. We are in a real battle against a real enemy. We must be on guard and live our lives pleasing to the one and only true God, God Almighty. His Son the Lord Jesus Christ is the only Savior of sinners of which we were in times past. We must remember how Blessed we are or the blessings could cease to be. The blessings we are enjoying right now whether natural or spiritual, are the results of victories won by men and women who died winning the battle that you and I have never fought. Our Grandparents and our parents prayed to God for us that He would have mercy on us and our children, and that we would be a people bringing Glory to His name by the lives that we live for Him.

Have you ever taken time to think about the many privileges we have enjoyed as citizens of the United State of America during our lifetime? We are living on the ground that has been soaked in the blood of those who have engaged in battle for this present victory we now enjoy. They in effect declared give me liberty or give me death! If you have surrendered your life to Christ, you have been given the authority to declare; give me liberty because of death! That is the death of so many of our fellow men and women, and ultimately the death that Jesus our lord experienced for us! The shedding of His blood is the foundation on which our salvation stands, which accomplishes our physical victories as well as the spiritual ones. The following elements were the key to this victory won by our Savior on behalf of mankind. They are Beauty, agony, death and life.

"For unto us a child is born, unto us a son is given: and the government shall be upon his shoulder..." Isaiah 9:6 (KJV)

The Prophet Isaiah foretold of the coming Messiah who would bring salvation to men, Jesus the Christ of God.

Jesus had a purpose He was destined to fulfill, and there could be no substitutes. The way for Him to achieve this victory was already set before the foundation of the world, and there would be no detours. Because of Jesus we have a purpose, and there must also be no detours with us. Detours, whether natural or spiritual, will take you a different way from which you were headed; they can also keep you from coming to realize your purpose. A life without purpose is like a misguided missile, someone is either going to get hurt or killed unless something is done to change its course.

Jesus' purpose was to live a life of selfless service bringing people to this victory He has won for us. This victory would not come easy for Him, but it would surely come. The cross would be no hindrance for the joy and victory to come afterward.

Jesus' enemies fought Him with hopes that He would abort His mission. That would not happen; He would surely win this victory. And because He won, we win! He fought to get this victory for us, and now if we would win in this our Christian walk we must fight!

"Fight the good fight of faith, take hold of eternal life...." I Timothy 6:12 (NIV)

Beauty

"I am the Rose of Sharon, and the Lily of the valley.
As the Lily among thorns is my love among the daughters.
As the apple tree among the trees of the wood, so is my beloved among the sons. I sat down under His shadow with great delight, and His fruit was sweet to my taste." Song of Solomon 2:1-3 (KJV)

This Song of Solomon with its twofold reference describes a lover singing of the purity and beauty of his beloved. It is also a reference to the love which Christ has for His Church. The beauty of the spotless Heavenly flower, the one who had no blemish, could have chosen to stay within the Heavenly place. But He took off as it were His royal and priestly garments and came to earth, and becoming a man, He would experience the shame and degradation of sinners. He came not for any fame, but solely to redeem mankind.

He demonstrated a depth of love that has never been equaled by any throughout all time. How beautiful is that?

You may have heard the saying that "beauty is only skin deep". That statement is really saying; remove the skin and there is no beauty. People can have an attractive outward appearance, but the real beauty of a person is found on the inside. The beauty that Jesus exhibited was not just surface beauty. The real beauty of a person is designed by God to be expressed in their character and the attitude of the heart. As a child of God, when you walk into a room, others should notice this beauty, which is designed to affect others for good. It is beauty which shines from the light of Christ in you.

Others may not be able to explain what makes them notice our entrance, but beyond the physical appearance they should sense the beauty of Christ in us. This beauty comes as a reflection of spending quality time in the presence of the Lord. Real beauty is the love of God. There has been no greater expression of this beauty than when our Lord Jesus showed it to the world by dying on the Cross to take away our sins. He who is eternal came and died for those who are temporal, so that we who are temporal might be with him for eternity. God's love for us and his love in us is the real beauty of a person.

Isaiah saw in a vision this beauty as the train of God's robe of glory filled the temple in Jerusalem.

*"In the year that King Uzziah died, I saw the Lord sitting on a throne, high and lifted up, and the train of His robe **filled the temple...**" Isaiah 6:1a (KJV)*

The power of Jesus' love parallels his glory. The brightness of that glory of which no man can approach unto, he concealed for a time and walked among us to show us His love for humanity. Look at how He expressed the greatest love for a world of dying sinners. In dying He saved us, when He arose, He justified us, He presently stands before our Heavenly Father interceding for us, and soon He will *return for us.*

"Greater love has no one than this, than to lay down one's life for his friends." *John 15:13 (NKJV)*

This is love that we may never fully understand while we are in this world. It was love that paid the ultimate price. What could even come close to being as beautiful as this?

Agony

Agony is a word that the Christian Church can relate to. It is spoken frequently in the scriptures. The Church began in the midst of persecution which for some resulted in pain and agony for holding to their faith. It's a word that no one is excited about, but it is the way in which we sometimes triumph in the Christian life.

"If we suffer with Him, we shall reign with Him." Romans 8:17

The way to eternal life is not always easy, and Jesus never promised us that it would be. Keeping our own flesh subdued is often our biggest challenge. *If we mortify (kill) the deeds of the body, we shall live – Romans 8:13. Sometimes that feels like agony.*

In Webster's dictionary, the definition for the word agony is divided into three parts. I will save the first part for last. The second part is - "Intense pain of mind and body." The third part is - "The struggle that precedes death." But I found the first part of the definition rather interesting. It is "Contest for a prize, to lead, celebrate".

Intense pain of mind and body was what Jesus felt as He drew nearer to the cross. But despite the agony He looked ahead and strove as one contesting for the prize. The greatness of Jesus' love for us was stronger the pain of agony. I'm glad He understood that suffering was the only way to bring deliverance to His people.

You and I may not be called to experience agony to the extent that Jesus did, but we do suffer now and then as we bear a cross.

As we find patience and comfort in the scriptures, we get God's direction for our lives, and we realize that our suffering is never in vain in the Lord. In dying on the cross and rising from the grave Jesus is the first begotten from the dead, and the first fruit of the resurrection. Because of His triumph over death, Hell and the grave, everyone who receives Him as Lord and Savior will share in His victory. The results for all who follow Him will be eternal life, having put to death the old nature and being raised to new life.

While Jesus carried His cross to the hill of Golgotha, some people in the crowd spit on Him, others struck Him on the cheek, and others flogged Him. Since He has suffered for all for us, He can relate to all of us. Sometimes in life other people may hurt us and we find it difficult to press on. But Jesus has felt what we feel. He can relate to unfair treatment from others, and He knows what it's like to be broken or cast aside. Although agony was part of the price of redemption, this was the way He chose to redeem men back to God. No matter how intense the agony, victory was a sure thing and nothing could keep him from it.

Death
(The Dark Night of the Soul)

I don't know anyone who enjoys talking about death, but it really is the starting point on the road to eternal life. I'm not talking about literal death only, but death to the ways of the flesh, which allows The Holy Spirit access to accomplish His work within us. The apostle Paul had found the key to advance in his spiritual life when he said…

"For when I am weak, then am I strong." II Corinthians 12:10b (KJV)

The Apostle could say this because he had learned that the secret to successfully walk with Christ required the yielding of the total man, yielding every fiber of his being to Christ. So, his flesh could not rule over his spirit, nor the outcome of his life.

Almost every one of my friends who are in ministry, whether they are Pastors or laity; they speak to me of times in their lives when they passed through feelings of deep despair, at times when it seemed like God had forsaken them. This is what our Lord Jesus experienced in the Garden of Gethsemane just before the Sanhedrin leaders sent the soldiers to apprehend him. This situation is the place described by many as "The dark Night of the soul;" the place where we find ourselves on the front line of spiritual warfare. It is the place where everything about us is tested to our limit to see whether we will go backward, stand still, or go forward.

"And being in agony, He prayed more earnestly, and His sweat was, as it were, great drops of blood falling down to the ground." Luke 22:24 (KJV)

The events of the above scripture took place in the Garden of Gethsemane, located at the foot of the Mount of Olives in Jerusalem, the place that is now famous as the place where Jesus prayed while his disciples slept. It was the night prior to His flogging and trial leading up to his crucifixion. Under the pressure and constraint of the flesh not wanting to feel the pains of crucifixion He agonized in the garden just before the soldiers came and took Him before the Magistrates.

We may never fully understand the kind of love that was willing to experience such horrific suffering for mankind. No doubt, Jesus prayed earnestly because He knew the power of fervent prayer. He teaches us that *"Men aught always to pray and not to faint." Luke 18:1(KJV)*

Prayer can bring an answer to anything that arises in our lives. The book of Psalms also gives us a description of the effectual fervent prayer.

"Deep calls unto deep at the noise of your waterspouts: all your waves and your billows are gone over me. Yet the Lord will command his loving kindness in the daytime, and in the night His song shall be with me, and my prayer unto the God of my life." Psalm 42:7-8 (KJV)

The above Psalm was written by Israel's beloved King David. The cry of his Prophetic writings foreshadowed the sufferings of the coming of Jesus the Lamb of God. This verse is a reference to Luke 22:24 of Jesus' agony just before going to the Cross to suffer for all humanity. He fulfilled this Prophetic cry while in the Garden of Gethsemane as His experienced the *"dark night of the soul"*. This was the place of brokenness where "deep calleth unto deep" The deepness of the soul of man touching the deepness of the heart of God and placing a demand upon God's supply.

This is the place in our lives where we sometimes experience no apparent response from God, in the silence of God; and where we share in the fellowship of Jesus' suffering.

As Christians, our experiences mirror our Savior's experiences, and in drinking of the same cup with Him we are made partakers of the suffering which identifies us with Christ.

"For our light affliction, which is but for a moment, worketh for us a far more exceeding and eternal weight of glory; …" II Corinthians 4:17 (KJV)

Praise be to God that the suffering of Jesus in the Garden was only a prelude to the final victory to be won. And what a victory it was! All of Heaven and earth rejoiced at His triumph over death, hell and the grave, while Satan and the powers of darkness trembled at what had just taken place.

Our dark night sometimes comes in the course of waiting patiently for the Lord to answer our prayers, or the times when our dreams seem to be delayed, and He doesn't answer us when or how we think he should. These are places and times where the enemy brings darkness around us and tries to discourage us. But we can take courage in knowing that God's Word is within us, and what He has purposed for our lives will not return to Him void; it will be accomplished. He is still in control and His plans for you and me will be realized because He never fails. As we look beyond our momentary sufferings with hope and faith in Jesus our victorious Savior; we know that because of what He has done, at the end we will declare with Him; we win!

"Weeping may endure for a night, but joy cometh in the morning." Psalm 30:5 (KJV)

Our Lord Jesus had no sins, yet He suffered in the flesh. Observe the extent of His great passion for the souls of men. In denying the desire of His flesh ("If you are willing, let this cup pass") He showed to us that victory over the limitations of the flesh is achievable for everyone. As He prayed it was spiritual warfare raging on the inside between His Spirit and His flesh.

The first thing to know in spiritual warfare is who's in charge. Jesus was aware of His own strength, and that the battled belonged to God, not to the flesh, and not to Satan. Knowing who's in charge makes all the difference in the outcome of our battles.

Jesus chose not to run away from the fight, He knew that His Father had equipped Him for this confrontation. He was equipped with The Truth, with Righteousness, The Gospel of Peace, The shield of Faith, and He was clad with the power of Salvation. Read *Ephesians 6:10-18*, for more on being equipped for spiritual warfare.

At the end of Jesus' prayer, He concluded with *"Nevertheless, not my will but thy will be done." Luke 22:42 (ESV)*

After resisting the cry of His flesh, it was settled. From here it was on to victory!

This speaks volumes to you and I that out of death (to the ways of flesh) comes life in the Spirit. Jesus can relate to our weaknesses, and He knows our limitations because He has experienced what we experience every day. He is able and ready to help us in our time of need. He is wise, He knows what the end will be before it comes. His ways are past finding out, and His love is greater than we could ever imagine.

Jesus You're Late!

"Now Jesus loved Martha and her sister and Lazarus, so when he heard that he (Lazarus) was sick, he stayed two more days in the place where he was." John 11:5-6 (KJV)

This story of Martha, Mary and Lazarus reminds us that at times Jesus may not answer a prayer at the time we think He will. His answer may not come on our schedule, but He will answer us.

The question here is, if Jesus loved them, why would he remain in the place where He was for two more days after hearing of Lazarus' sickness? It is noteworthy to say that if he had gone earlier Lazarus would still have been alive; and the people there would not have witnessed the display of God's supernatural power which gives men life again.

How many times have we said the same thing as Martha and Mary? Lord if you only had shown up sooner, things would have been different. They were saying *Jesus you're late!* Or was He?

Have you ever asked the question, what was Jesus doing while death was knocking at their door? Well Jesus always has a plan and a reason for every action He takes on behalf of His people. He could have rushed on his way and gotten there just in the knick of time. He could have even stayed where He was and simply spoke the word and Lazarus would have remained alive. What was He doing? It appears that Jesus was just *letting the flesh die.*

For those times when Jesus doesn't show up for us when we want Him to, it may be that He is just letting the flesh die. As we cooperate with Him in doing His will we mortify (put to death) the deeds of the flesh, and give The Holy Spirit unhindered access to raise us up to greater places of service in Christ.

Jesus cried out on the cross "my God, my God, why have you forsaken me?" He was not guilty of any sin, but God the Father did not answer His cry from the cross because He was *letting the flesh die,* thereby, allowing the Spirit to accomplish the great work of salvation.

Sometimes the Lord Jesus may not give us the answer to a prayer, remove an obstacle; or give us the why of a situation until something dies first. I mean in those areas in our lives where the flesh has to be brought under subjection to the power of the Holy Spirit. The truth is, according to the scriptures, if we would be strong spiritually, we must become weak as Paul declared, *"when I am weak then am I strong." II Corinthians 12:10b*

Here Paul the Apostle had found the key to a prosperous and successful Christian life and ministry. If we want to get off the ground (so to speak) and to become successful in our personal lives and ministry for Christ, we must remember that Gethsemane (the proving ground of our faith) must be the launching pad. Jesus' body experienced great struggle and pains in Gethsemane while the cross awaited Him. It seemed like more than the flesh could endure. But His struggles in Gethsemane, "this dark night of the soul" would confirm whether the ministry He had established would remain in the hearts of those whom He had transformed. The pressures brought forth the test for His decision to trust his father and His commitment to His mission.

Our commitment to the Lord will always be tested while we wait for His promises to us, and while we are looking for that dream that he has given to us.

Satan our enemy and adversary of God wants to steal our God-given dreams, and to destroy our vision. But dreams and visions that are given by God are the property of God, therefore they cannot be thwarted. If that dream has really been given to you by God, it will be bigger than you, and something that you cannot do in your own strength. It will be something that God alone can accomplish by His own power through you as you yield to him in total submission.

As we give ourselves to Him with complete submission to His will, this place "The dark night of the soul" is where we experience new life out of a death situation, rising to new heights in Christ that we have never known before. This is a figurative resurrection, a foreshadowing of that literal resurrection which is to come.

Jesus experienced the victory after death to the flesh. The dark night of the soul gave way to the Day light of the Spirit!

Life
Let the Fashion Show Begin

"In the beginning God created the heavens and the earth." Genesis 1:1 (KJV)

In this verse, the Hebrew form of the word created is **"Bara"** (Heb) which denotes forming something from nothing; while in verse twenty-six of this same chapter, the word made is **"Asah"** (Heb) which has more to do with fashioning the created object.

In this section, I want to focus on being fashioned; and to compare the fashioning process to being formed and shaped into the likeness of Christ. Since eternal life will be our ultimate reward at the end of our Christian walk, I want to bring you to the realization that the rewards we will receive after suffering for Christ, far outweigh the pains of fashioning. So, let the fashion show begin.

For any fashion show to be a success, certain things must first be put in place. First of all, you will need someone with a vision, a concept, a plan. Next you will need a designer, one who can transform the idea into a pattern, which is followed by the literal design, making the vision a reality. What began as only a thought in the mind of the creator/designer has become a reality. Now they need people to put on and model their product. Designers hire only people who will complement their product when worn, while at the same time the product makes the model look good. Now if you're going to model the wardrobe you'll be wearing, you can't just eat everything that your palate craves. There has to be some discipline involved or you're not going to fit into that dress or suit.

Now I know that in the fashion world, our culture has shaped our minds into thinking that a real model only fits into a perfect six. But my focus is not on extremes, I'm just making a physical and spiritual comparison.

God's plan for our lives is to model his Son in all that we say and do, which also calls for discipline, Dieting right, and other necessary preparations. In the fashion world, when these things are not practiced the model will not be up to the task and is likely to blow it while on the runway. The prospective buyers observing the models on the runway know what to look for, such as any flawed garments, and the highest quality among other things. Since this is a prospective investment for them, they want to avoid wasting time or resources. As they watch the models, they are actually seeing the heart, mind and soul of the one who created the product.

Jesus has invested too much into you and I to allow our flaws, imperfections or weaknesses to degrade our prospect of Heaven.

Like in the fashion world; and more so with Jesus, only the best and nothing less will do. Wearing His name means we represent Him.

"By this all men will know that you are my Disciples, if you have love one for another." John 13:35

The way that people know whose product it is on the runway is by the signature of the creator/designer. It is the same when it comes to living for Christ. The only way that other people will know that we are disciples of Jesus Christ is by our love for each other. Nothing else gets people's attention like love, because everyone wants to be loved. The most hardened of hearts, though calloused it may be, wants to be loved. God's love is the language of life, and life is incomplete without it. When other people see us, they should see Jesus, as they get to know us, they should have a sense of who He is by the love that we show them.

After the fashion show, the images and designs remain in the minds of the observers long after the models have left the runway. The models have left an impression on the observers.

Showing God's love to everyone, we meet leaves lasting impressions on them, especially on those who are poor, outcast, unloved and downtrodden. It is here where the world can see through the models (you and I) the heart, mind and soul of our creator/designer who is Jesus Christ.

Have you ever asked yourself the question how do other people see me? I do. What happens with people who have been around us for a while? They may have spoken some nice things about us while in our presence, but when they have left the room; do they have a clear perception of us that we are followers of Christ? Perception is everything. Our lives should be models for Christ before the world as we share God's love. We bear the image of Jesus because we are His workmanship by design; created for Him to do good works.

"For we are his workmanship, created in Christ Jesus unto good works, which God hath before ordained that we should walk in them." Ephesians 2:10 (KJV)

We are a work in progress.

For millennia God has been fashioning models from the runways of Heaven, dressed in apparel that is glorious; created to be on display for eternity.

The Patriarchs in Old Testament times were models to represent to the world the awesomeness of Almighty God. Now in New Testament times through the Church is revealed the beauty of Jesus the Christ. He has chosen you and I as He fashions us into models of His love that He might receive an end time harvest of souls into His Kingdom. Because of His great sacrifice of love His Kingdom comes on earth as it is in Heaven. It was an awesome sacrifice that Jesus made when He purchased our salvation on Calvary's cross. He did not have to do it, but He chose to suffer in our place; it was the ultimate sacrifice.

Sometimes winning others to Him may call for an inconvenience or a sacrifice of some kind, but ours can never compare to His. He has poured out His heart, soul and literally Himself to redeem us and He wants to be at the center of what we say and do. His desire is to shape our lives through a process that builds our faith that we may be fashioned more and more into his likeness.

Chapter 5

Seasons of Change
(The In-Between Factor)

"There is a time for everything, and a season for every activity under the heavens." Ecclesiastes 3:1(NIV)

In this section of the book, we will deal with what I call "The In between Factor". It consists of (1) coming into unfamiliar places in your walk with Christ, (2) getting stuck, (3) then learning to make the change or transition on to new levels of service for Him. And (4) It will also encourage us on what we must do while we are waiting in the dry season.

Everybody is familiar with change. It happens in route from one place to another. The world operates on change. It is a natural part of life. The truth is, life is all about change. In fact, anyone who tries to live life without it finds themselves not really living at all; because in God's creation everything changes. Normal to life, it is sometimes easy to make a change, while at other times it is a challenge. But depending on the kind of change, it can be a healthy asset to life. The natural seasons give us one of the clearest examples of change. Every season brings certain things with them. Each one is unique in that they are known by the contrast associated with them. Spring is known for beginning anew, like a fresh start. Summer is known by the heat it brings, signifying that the season is now at its peak. Fall is the decline of the season, shedding itself of what now is old and not usable anymore. The coming of winter is known by the cold that it brings. The cold kills off all signs of the old and prepares the ground for planting seeds for a future harvest. As it is with the natural seasons, so it is with the seasons of our lives. Change is designed by God, and each change is aimed at improvement. It has been said that the only easy way to deal with change is when you are the one doing the change. But we are not always in control of the changes we experience in life. As followers of Christ, we are dwellers on earth but citizens of Heaven. Our salvation was purchased with the shed blood of Jesus Christ, so we belong to Him; and we don't always know the right and best changes that need to be made. Granted, we make changes according to what we think is best, but the Lord may interrupt the ones we make to implement His own, bringing to us a challenge to make the adjustment. In each stage of life, we learn to adjust, being conscious of this truth; that with the adjustment we are being shaped more into the image of Christ. The point of change is the doorway to broader fields of service which brings with it higher levels of glory. The Christian life is designed so that each change will enable us to excel to new heights of maturity in Christ. You see, change is necessary for progress and growth. When one changes their mind, they will change their life. When one changes their course, their direction is changed. Change your life, and you will change your destiny. The Bible is filled with verses and accounts of change.

In Genesis Chapter 37 Joseph experienced drastic change when he was betrayed by his brothers and sold into slavery. But in later years the Lord turned the tide, and Joseph ended up becoming the governor of all the land of Egypt, becoming Pharaoh's right-hand man. He was changed because his God was with him, and God was the one making the changes.

"God is not man, that he should lie, or a son of man, that he should change his mind. Has he said, and will he not do it? Or has he spoken, and will he not fulfill it?" Numbers 23:19 (NIV)

Stuck in a Season

"I waited patiently for the Lord; and He inclined to me, and heard my cry.

He also brought me up out of a horrible pit, out of the miry clay, and set my feet upon a rock, and established my steps.

He has put a new song in my mouth, Praise to our God; Many will see it and fear, and will trust in the Lord." Psalm 40:1-8 (KJV)

Have you ever gotten stuck in a season? What do you do when you're stuck in a season? When you are in a hot and dry season, everything changes.

Thankfully, one of the greatest things about God's love for us and His faithfulness is that it never wanes and it is never affected by our spiritual dry season. So don't worry during those times, you are not alone, every child of God goes through them. But dry seasons are often used by God to challenge and to build strong faith in us.

Psalm 40 is a Psalm of deliverance; describing what comes after the test, trial or challenge to our faith. It reveals to us the reward that comes to those who are willing to put their trust in the Lord and wait patiently for Him.

David is the writer of this Psalm. The order of his dilemma was: He began, he waited and then he was rewarded. Now take note that his waiting preceded the reward. The reward is the result of the waiting.

Our lives are filled with changes, transitions, times and seasons which begin and end. Some seasons are short, others are longer, but none of them are designed to last forever.

The waiting and the reward are two important factors in this scenario, but the time spent between the two is crucial to the final victory.

The waiting time is the process needed to get us through. In a word – our proper response in the waiting time of a spiritual dry season to a great degree determines our victory.

It is not surprising that the Lord makes promises to us that are not always quickly executed. Sometimes, and my experience has been that most of the time, we must wait.

First of all, there are no seasons without purpose. God has designed them with you and I in mind. The most important thing is not that these seasons come, but rather what we do with them when they come. There are seasons of light, and seasons of darkness, seasons where we cruise right on through. We go through seasons that are not so easy; and there are others when we even get stuck and we need a little help. The Lord has the Divine prescription for what ails us in each life season. As the physical seasons are natural parts of life, more so the spiritual ones. Each one is different. And one that doesn't give way to the next one signifies that something is wrong. Hence, the ones in the season are not getting the desired benefit out of it.

What if winter remained 365 days a year, 365 days of snow?

Or what if there were 365 days of 98 degrees of hot weather?

It can be explained in one word. Miserable!

Well, that's what our spiritual season is like when it doesn't change or doesn't change on time.

The State of Alaska's year is fascinating. Alaska is the Northern most state leading up to the North Pole. Everything above the Arctic Circle gets about 67 straight nights of darkness in the winter, and about 80 straight days of sun light in the summer. How's that for being stuck in a long season?

God is the Master mind behind how it is all designed. At creation (Genesis Chapters 1 and 2) God designed the natural earth and made it to be conducive for mankind. Will He not also provide for him spiritually as well? Yes, He will, after all He has declared that *"All souls are mine"* according to the book of *Ezekiel Chapter 18 verse 4.*

King David was a man who was no stranger to life's seasons of change and challenge. In fact, his writings are among some of the most profound and encouraging in the scriptures. They bring us comfort in times of trouble. David admonishes us in *Psalm Chapter 27 verse 14* to *"wait on the Lord, be of good courage, and He shall strengthen your heart"*. Then he repeats it by saying: *"wait I say on the Lord"* which signifies – don't be mistaken, God will surely strengthen you if you are willing to wait for Him.

What about your season? What's happening in your seasons of life, and how do you handle them? Do you pretend that they don't exist?

Or, do you act as some others do; as if you are the only one going through it? As I stated previously, we all go through them. You are not alone! David's experiences help to strengthen us in such times.

Through King David's experiences, he learned the lesson that consistency brings. He got a handle on "Stick–to–it-iveness".

He stuck to the fight until what he was waiting for came to pass; being convinced that seasons are designed to change!!!

Going through your season with the above reminder will enable you to become unstuck and become productive while passing through on your way to victory.

Personally, I believe that if the Lord's Church was ever in a dry or dark season it is now. Spiritual, moral and social-economical decay has been the conditions of the Church and the world for the last few decades. Somewhere along the way we got stuck. But God has provided us a way through! When we get stuck, we don't just sit there. We get into God's Word for guidance to find our way out. There is a purpose behind every obstacle that happens to be in front of us. God has a plan, so we must not stop, but keep pressing forward as He carries us on to the next level of maturity by His Grace. Everything and everyone have a beginning and an end, and nothing finishes like it starts. Between the start and the finish transition takes place.

My aim in this section is to focus on the in between activity, the transition we experience as we grow from one level of grace to another while living for Christ.

In the book of Galatians Chapter 4 verse 19 the Apostle Paul pours out his heart to them as he shares his desire to see Christ formed in them. He also understood that this would take time and effort to accomplish. In order for Christ to be form in us it takes time, and if we would be successful in getting all that the Lord wants for us in transition it is needful to know the things required. The Bible talks to us about a vision in *Proverbs 29:18*. It says… *"Where there is no vision, the people perish…"*

To have a vision actually prepares us for the transition, because a vision is made up of (1) seeing the goal (2) going through the process to attain it, and (3) finally reaching the goal. The one who has the vision is known as the visionary. A visionary at the beginning sees their vision as finished; with the anticipation of getting from point A to point B.

When God speaks a word to you, or shows you things to come, it is normal to be excited with anticipation. You've gotten His Word on it (which is the beginning of it), you envision it in its completeness, (you can see the end of it), but the in-between factor; the transition is more important than the start or the finish, because the transition is the main element of it all. Now and then our Christian journey requires transition out of us. As God leads us, the when and how of our transition is also crucial, because the transition itself is the meat of the process. Transition requires hard work. Sometimes in transition it will appear that most things are working against us, but we can't be fooled by that. Opposition is not our enemy. In fact, the absence of trouble is no indicator that all will be well. Some of my most impacting breakthroughs and some of my greatest victories were realized while trouble was knocking at my door. Transition has its Pros and Cons.

While we transition into new things it is easy to be deceived into despising the day of small things. Read *(Zechariah 4:10)*. But small things are a natural part of life. They are often used as the springboard for great works of God in life; right in those places where at the first it looked like we had nothing to work with. Observe this; Even before The Lord Himself spoke the Words *"Let there be light" (Gen. 1:3)* there was nothing there to work with.

When in a transition our perspective is everything. How we get through it is just as important as that we get through it. Our attitude about things plays a prominent role in it all, which will determine whether we are successful. Our attitude is examined by the Lord as He takes us through uncharted areas, and regions of new experiences in Him.

In Romans Chapter 4 verse 17, Paul restates the words of the Lord to Abraham in *Genesis 17:4-5;* which says *(As it is written, I have made thee a father of many nations,) before him whom he believed, even God, who quickens the dead, and calls those things which be not as though they were.*

The CJB (Complete Jewish Bible) agrees with the *Tanakh,* which is the Canonical collection of Jewish texts, where it says…

"I have appointed you to be a father to many nations."

Abraham is our spiritual father according to (Romans 4:12).

If we trust God as he did; we will be convinced that God is the one who gives life to the dead and calls nonexistent things into existence. Notice the Transition… *"Your name shall no more be called Abram"* (Exalted Father)…but Abraham (Father of many) (Genesis 17:5).

It is evident that God had the power to change Abram's name, but the name change was not the element of transition, on the contrary, the name change was simply the result of it.

Genesis 7:2 shows us that it was the covenant which God had made with Abraham that was the agent of transition. So, Abraham accepted God's Words, and caught the vision of it, accepting it as done! From now on he and his descendants would be in transition throughout the balance of their years here on earth.

What is most important here is that God was in control of the whole process of Abraham's rise or transition to the status of "Father of many Nations".

Transitions

"Be strong and of a good courage: for unto this people you shall divide for an inheritance the land." Joshua 1:6a (KJV)

"For who hath despised the day of small things? For they shall rejoice, and shall see the plummet in the hand of Zerubbabel with those seven." Zechariah 4:10a (KJV)

In both of the above scriptures God's people are in a period of transition. In the book of Joshua Israel prepares to enter their promise land for the first time, while in Zechariah's book Israel has returned to the promise land after being in captivity for seventy years to the Babylonians. The key word linking the two books together is "Transition". Transition means to transverse, to move. It is the process or a period of changing from one state or condition to another.

Since the dawning of creation God has been on the scene and behind the scenes causing transitions that fulfill His purpose in the lives of men and women. He has guided the footsteps of mankind from Old Testament times up through New Testament times.

The Nation of Israel had been chosen as the first post flood family of the earth to show forth the splendor of Jehovah; and the family through whom God would send the Messiah. This transition had begun at the borders of the land of Caanan.

Significant transition began with the Nation of Israel. Lots of changes took place in the life of the Nation before entering the land. God's hand of guidance had been upon them from their very inception. Their beginning was small, but their finish would be grand.

That finish depended solely upon their obedience in living according to God's Word. This was God's instructions to them:

Yes, keep this book of the Torah on your lips, and meditate on it day and night, so that you will take care to act according to everything written in it. Then your undertakings will prosper, and you will succeed - Joshua 1:8 CJB (Complete Jewish Bible).

During the times of Zechariah, the people of Israel now back in their homeland were given a second chance to make things right in their relationship with their God.

Zechariah's task was to encourage his people to move with the changes the Lord God was making in their lives. His people were on the precipice of drastic change, and they could not afford to miss the mark this time. Their job was to believe and to trust in God, because this would be their last great conquest to rebuild the city of Jerusalem, and the Temple before the entrance of the age of Messiah.

They would rebuild, and in a few centuries, Messiah would come; this was His promise because they were His Covenant people.

Obedience to God's Word guaranteed the prosperity and success of His people back then, and so it guarantees ours today.

They learned to move with God. Herein lies our victory, our hopes and dreams, the answers to our prayers, our satisfaction and contentment in life.

You may be in a transition right now? Well for us to get the full benefits of the transition, we must be established upon the terms on the covenant. You may ask, what Covenant?

We have been grafted into the family of God and to a Covenant relationship with Jesus Christ - *I say then, Have they (The Jews) stumbled that they should fall? God forbid: but rather through their fall salvation is come unto the Gentiles, for to provoke them to jealousy. Now if the fall of them be the riches of the world, and the diminishing of them the riches of the Gentiles; how much more their fullness? Romans 11:11-12 (KJV).* Transition is always good when God initiates it.

It is a thrill and an honor to think that God would consider you and I to be part of this great work of Kingdom building for Him.

Although it is exciting as we look ahead by faith and see our vision as complete, our greatest task is learning to embrace the transition days and years of life, because in the transitions is where we are armed for the battles of life, and where we are equipped for whatever lies ahead of us. It is in this place where dreams are realized and visions are fulfilled.

From personal experience, I don't believe it is possible to realize the value of a fulfilled dream or vision without first learning to appreciate the course, the journey, and the transition on the way to it.

Nothing or anyone on earth can be classified as productive without transition. Your Christian life and mine was created for it.

Children are born as babies, but they don't remain that way.

The New Year comes in as January, but it proceeds on to December.

The sun rises in the eastern sky and transitions to the west.

Notice that it never turns around to go in the opposite direction.

The Christian life is not meant to be lived in an oscillating (Back and forth) transition, but we are designed by God to make transitions which last for eternity. We must declare that from here we go onward and upward as we transition in our Christian walk.

I believe God is about to make radical changes in His Church and to bring times of revival and renewal. It is a time for us to re-connect, re-assess, and to re-commit ourselves to Him. The change He brings comes with the purpose of improving and making us more like Him. In these times in which we live, the condition of people's lives calls for national repentance throughout the Nations. Repentance means to turn, or turn away from sin with regret and remorse; literally to change directions. The day when we learn to change our mind (repent) and follow in the footsteps of Jesus Christ will be the day when our spiritual growth rises to new heights of maturity that we have not known before.

"And be not conformed to this world: but be ye transformed [changed] by the renewing of your mind, that ye may prove what is that good, and acceptable, and perfect, will of God." Romans 12:2 (KJV)

When we do this, we will be reminded that God always does what He has promised.

Here are some words of encouragement that will help and keep us active, along with scriptures; to strengthen us in being productive on the way to our victory.

When you're stuck in a season:

1. Erase the word limits off your list. *The Lord's hand is not shortened that He cannot save you. (Isaiah 59:1)*
2. Be completely honest yourself. Examine your own heart to see if there is anything in it that would prevent a move of God in your life. *Read Psalm 66:18* (regarding Iniquity).

3. Bring your complaint to God and not to people as King David did. *(I cried unto the Lord…poured out my complaint to Him (Psalm 27).* God knows what season you are in, and He knows what time it is in your life.
4. Don't isolate yourself, stay in fellowship with other believers…. Read *Hebrews 10:25.*
   Also, keep good Communication with other people - Read *Hebrews 13:16.*
5. Don't lean on your own understanding *("…and He shall direct your paths," Read Proverbs 3:6).*

Remember what I shared with you earlier concerning Alaska's days and nights? Be encouraged by this. Even after 67 nights of darkness in Alaska; the light eventually breaks through, and the Alaskans enjoy the light of the sun again. You are only in a season! And this too shall pass! Then the dawn shall break! Day light is Coming, and you will make the transition into a new level of grace.

Escape from Your Comfort Zone

"Now there is at Jerusalem by the sheep market a pool, which is called in the Hebrew tongue Bethesda, having five porches.

And a certain man was there, which had an infirmity thirty and eight years.

When Jesus saw him lie, and knew that he had been now a long time in that case, he saith unto him, Wilt thou be made whole?

The impotent man answered him, Sir, I have no man, when the water is troubled, to put me into the pool: but while I am coming, another steppeth down before me.

Jesus saith unto him, Rise, take up thy bed, and walk." John 5:2;5-8 (KJV).

The above story took place in Jerusalem. The five porches spoken of are part of the Temple at Jerusalem. The section of the Temple where Jesus heals the man is called "Solomon's Greatly Wondering", it is a place associated with healing (read Acts 3:11).

We can compare some of our life situations and encounters with this man's dilemma. Life situations can sometimes work against us. They have a way of hindering us from accomplishing our God-given goals. After Jesus commands him to rise, He says "Take up thy bed".

Our bed is what we lie upon each night. It is an instrument that is designed for comfort, ease and rest.

It is a good thing to have in your possession. Some people sleep on their sides; others are more comfortable lying on their back. Some people are even able to rest lying on their stomach. Whatever suits you best, if it works, sleep!

But when it comes to spiritual things the place of lounging and relaxing just may not be the best place to be in. Although Jesus gives us seasons of comfort and rest, it is not to be expected everyday out of our year.

We would only speculate anything beyond what the scripture says about this man. But perhaps after such a long time of waiting; could he have gotten used to just lying there by the pool? Maybe he just accepted his plight; hoping that he would get healed but becoming comfortable at his station in life. Have you ever been there?

Our comfort zone is the place that we've gotten used to, and the place where we put forth the least effort. It is the place where we feel safe from having to respond to whatever may be required of us.

Our comfortable place in this Christian walk can be the place where we so easily put off praying until tomorrow, or when there is a need; we say I don't feel like it today, there are others who can do it, let them do it. But we cannot afford to become too comfortable at any time on our Christian journey.

Can you imagine waiting for something for 38 years? Surely this man had a story to tell about waiting. I'm not saying that this man was actually comfortable lying by the pool for thirty-eight years, but I'm sure he had gotten used to it.

What do you think, and what do you see when you read the scripture about his dilemma? Some have suggested that he should have found a way to get into the pool within the 38 years. Others say he was just too slow, and some say he didn't want it bad enough; and they go on and on with reasons why he was not healed.

But Jesus didn't dwell at all on the man's reason for being there for so long. He was more concerned about making the man whole. The man's faithful diligence brought him to the time when Jesus met Him there, literally right at the point of his need. While persevering he waited until his change finally came.

While in certain seasons of life waiting is the appropriate thing to do; perseverance in any season is always the needed thing to do.

Whether this man had gotten comfortable or just use to being in that position we don't know, but we do know that he needed to be delivered, and this was his moment. He needed something (in this case) someone to shake up his world.

Sometimes our world needs to get shaken up in order for us to break free from the comfortable place; that place where we have become (as it were) chained to. But it is amazing how a crisis can end up making us more effective servants for the Lord. And the Lord usually uses things, people and ways familiar to us to accomplish it. He starts with stirring up our faith.

We all have faith "…according as God hath dealt to every man the measure of faith." Romans 12:3c (KJV)

Regardless to the reason this man was there by the pool for so long, he had the recipe for his breakthrough within himself. He had at least three things that were working in his favor.

1. He believed he could be healed.
2. He was expecting to be healed.
3. He put no limit on time. It is apparent that he was not intimidated by the length of time which had passed. His breakthrough was now at hand.

Although he was looking for his breakthrough to appear in one way, it was about to happen in a totally different way, because God had a better way for him. When Jesus asked him, "do you want to be healed", it was not that Jesus didn't know if he did; it was to ignite the man's faith to believe for what Jesus was about to do.

Without hesitation the man responds - I want to, but I'm not physically quick enough to get into the pool before someone else gets in first (Paraphrase). He's really saying I can't do this with my own strength. Have you ever been there at the place of - I can't do this with my own strength? Well, I believe that sometimes that is exactly the place where the Lord is seeking to get us into. That is, the place where we finally acknowledge His Sovereignty, and our frailness and inability before Him. He has declared… *"Without me you can do nothing." John 15:5b (NKJV)*

We can see it throughout the scriptures that Jesus is able to shake up the normal flow of things in people's lives. He is able to get us out our comfort zone and into God's more excellent way for us.

"But covet earnestly the best gifts: and yet shew I unto you a more excellent way." I Corinthians 12:31 (AKJV)

Many times, we spend our lives trying to figure out what the Lord has already set up to happen in its time. The key element to receiving our petition is our consistency in waiting for Him.

Our victories are not won in a comfort zone, but in a battle zone.

While our leisure is apt to produce complacency, our battles assure opportunities for victory.

Ecclesiastes 5:3a says - *For a dream cometh through the multitude of business.* Simply put; in the midst of living out God's will for our lives, our dreams are realized.

In order to get the best out of life we must be up to the task of challenge! But the challenge is the sure-fire mechanism that gets us to our victory. So, let's take the challenge! When we do, we will find new avenues of life to walk through; with new heights and depths of God's grace through which we are armed for success in life.

When we are willing to press beyond our self-erected walls of false security; and explore the vastness of God's provision, life will yield to us unfathomable happiness, peace and contentment.

God's grace is provided fresh and new for us every morning.

So break out of that prison, and escape from your comfort zone!

Chapter 6

Wrestling with God

"And Jacob was left alone, and there a man wrestled with him until the daybreak. When the man saw that he could not defeat him, he struck Jacob's hip socket as they wrestled and dislocated his hip. Then he said to Jacob, let me go, for the day breaks. And he said, I will not let you go until you bless me." Genesis 32:24-26 (NIV)

What an encounter! After reading this story one cannot afford to miss the lesson it teaches us. What is happening here? It is evident that the man whom Jacob was wrestling with was no ordinary man. For why would he ask a man whom he was wrestling with to bless him?

Surely the one he wrestled with was not at all a man, but God.

You may say that the answer to that statement is a no brainer? No one wrestles with God and wins. But please allow me this luxury to rattle your cage a bit about that answer. In this scenario there is more than meets the eye. Allow me to explain.

Jacob's name was given the meaning "Holder of the heel", or "Supplanter" because twice he deprived his brother of his rights. He lived out the character of that name for many years. His character also causes many problems in his life; everything from being lied on, to being taken advantage of by relatives.

Because of his negative actions early on in life all these things had now come back to haunt him in later years. Through the course of Jacob's life, he got sidetracked for a while, but God would not allow these things to cause Jacob to miss His promises. This *"Wrestling with the man"* was a part of bringing to an end the things that would hinder Jacob's progress in achieving God's purpose, so The Lord began correcting what needed to be corrected in Jacob's life. The dilemma Jacob found himself in was leading up to a climax. This was not as much about a physical struggle, as it was about a spiritual struggle. Although by the end of this struggle Jacob would walk with a limp, the real struggle was with Jacob's heart, his mind set, his will, his emotions, his resolve and his spiritual condition before God. This event was the culmination or the peak of Jacob's lifestyle of trickery and deception. At this point in his life he had come to where he had to face his brother Esau, the same one whose birthright he had stolen. But before that would happen, God would cause Jacob to finally deal with his own past sins. He was now in what was probably the most desperate situation in his life, the place of not knowing what was going to happen to him. And besides all this, he now had a family of his own to protect from whatever his brother Esau might do. He was under lots of pressure, but his future depended on him getting it right this time.

Before the Lord would take Jacob into the next chapter of his life, He would need to get Jacob into his rightful place. He needed to clean up the places in his life that would hinder the fulfillment of God's promises made to him, his father and Grand Father. This was Jacob's defining moment. He was faced with one of two choices. He could stay the same way he had always been, or he could finally get serious about his life and persevere; arising out of that struggle into his rightful place in God as the Patriarch the Lord intended for him to be. This was a serious matter, because God's promises made to Abraham and Isaac also fell to Jacob. But the promise would not end with him, it would continue on to his descendants as well. In order for this to take effect, the Lord would first need to make some corrections in Jacob's life.

While living this Christian life we can also expect encounters with our Heavenly Father which brings us face to face with ourselves. That means anything that hinders our walk with our Lord, or anything that would threaten our relationship with Him must be dealt with directly and removed from our lives. The Lord's aim in doing so is to define to us who we really are, and so to move us into more effective service for Christ. He uses discipline, correction and chastisement despite the flawed nature of our flesh. Granted, the correction is not always easy for us to accept, but as we yield to the Savior's lead we begin to realize that this is actually the stuff which establishes the landmarks of our Christianity. It is in encounters like these where we are shaped, toughened and equipped so that as God uses us, He positions us to leave a legacy for future generations. Sure, there are times when we find ourselves in a situation like Jacob. But God can even use some things from our past to get us back on course in the process of preparing us for our future. And He can even work through the weak and flawed areas of our lives to accomplish it.

The Lord loved His servant Jacob. And as it was with Jacob, so it is with you and me. The Lord always corrects His own. The Bible calls it chastisement, of which all are partakers.

"And ye have forgotten the exhortation which speaketh unto you as unto children, My son, despise not thou the chastening of the Lord, nor faint when thou art rebuked of him: For whom the Lord loveth he chastens, and scourges every son whom he receives." Hebrews 12:5-6 (KJV)

Jacob was the biggest contributor to his failures. Sometimes our greatest threat to missing God's promise to us is ourselves, our own words and actions. In different areas of life, we sometimes struggle to break a habit we might have, or we battle to destroy a stronghold that has been set up in our life. This was the place Jacob had now come to. The place where only God alone could change things; and where he must wrestle with God to break the chains of "This is the way it has always been". It would not be easy for Jacob, but God would enable him to break free. And God will also enable you and I to break free.

"And he said unto him, what is your name? And he said, Jacob. And the man said, your name shall no more be called Jacob, but Israel: for as a prince you have power with God and with men, and have prevailed." Genesis 32:27-28 (KJV)

As it was with Jacob, so it must be with you and me. Whether in good times or bad; we cannot escape the consequences of our own actions. But beyond all these, God is still with us all the way confirming and performing His word.

It was time for Jacob to meet the conditions which allowed God's promises made to him to come to pass without hindrance. They were now long waiting. It was time for him to live out these promises, and he could only live them out God's way.

After this "wresting with God" was over Jacob finally learns that he cannot scheme his way through life any longer. He had to be accountable for his words and actions, and those consequences follow them. Jacob was now an overcomer. His challenges had proven to be blessings in disguise as they brought him to the reality of what the Lord required of him. He now had learned that prayers and perseverance toward his God was the key to all his victories in life.

"The effectual fervent prayer of a righteous man avails much." James 5:16b (KJV)

King David, Israel's celebrated and historic King was another man who had his share of suffering. But by prayer and perseverance he was always triumphant through his trials because he trusted in God.

"It was good for me to be afflicted so that I might learn your statutes." Psalm 119:71 (KJV)

I believe it takes a special kind of person, yes, a dedicated person to respond to trials in this way. We can relate to what David says in *Psalm 18:4 – "The sorrows of death surrounded me, and the floods of ungodly men made me afraid."*

But when have you or I ever prayed "it was good for me to be afflicted so that I might learn your statutes?" We want to learn His statues but without the afflictions.

Suffering Because of Sin

As I stated in the previous chapter, sometimes we can hinder our own progress. We are familiar with King David and God's favor on his life. We read about his many victories, and how he was granted the wisdom it takes to rule a kingdom. But we also read about his failures and mistakes; his folly and his foolishness, of which he paid a dear price. This caused him much sorrow. There is a big difference in suffering for the Lord's cause, and suffering for our own negligence and sins.

In the situation concerning Bathsheba, which takes up a huge part of David's life, he suffers for his own wrongdoings. This was a time in his life when he had blown it big time. By no means do we take lightly the matter of sin in anyone's life, and especially in our own. But I want to fast forward because my focus is not only on David's weakness and wrongdoing, but mainly on what the Lord did afterward.

First of all, David's reprimand was severe. David had to repent and make things right before his God. And no doubt there were people that he had to go back to and ask for forgiveness as well. On top of all this, although forgiven, he had to live with the shame that remained. But the point that I want to drive home is that after repentance and suffering the consequences of his actions, it was not all over for him.

There was still hope for him; the hope of arising and being restored to his relationship with God. God was not through with him. He could still be used by God after he had fallen into sin. Restoration was as close as repentance.

We cannot understand the depth of God's love for us that even after we make wrong choices, whether accidentally or deliberately; He is there ready to restore us if we will only sincerely repent.

King David is the writer of most of the Psalms in our Bible. Seventy-four of them are attributed to him. The Psalms are characteristic of and expressive to life experiences; and are adaptable by all humanity. David personified the Psalms by everyday experiences, our kind of experiences. Many of his writings powerfully relate to the feelings common to all believers of all times, intimately and personally relating to every human emotion.

"I have found David son of Jesse, a man after my own heart; he will do everything I want him to do." Acts 13:22 (KJV)

How could God say this about David after so many mess ups? The answer is simple; and almost hidden in plain sight. The answer is right there before our eyes in the verse.... *"he will do everything I want him to do". It was and still is all a matter of the heart. Are we willing to do everything He wants us to do?* Does this mean that you and I can be a man or woman after His heart? I believe it does. God's heart relates to every human experience. From deep despair to ecstatic delight; from a yearning for vengeance, to a spirit of humility and forgiveness; Jesus has experienced it all. He knows how and what to do in any given situation of your life and mine. David had many highs and lows in life, but he finally got it together and learned to live a disciplined life… making himself available to God.

What is the lesson for you and me in all this? It is this. Our suffering is not just about suffering. Suffering is not an end in itself. No, but it is a prelude to the favor and blessings that God has planned to place in our lives. Through His Word we have forgiveness for our sins, Hallelujah! You and I can begin again through the resurrection power of our risen Lord, our Savior Jesus Christ. In order for us to get the full benefit out of our suffering as God intends, we would do well to ourselves to have this same attitude as David; to do everything that The Lord wants us to do. Only then do we learn the real value of walking with Christ. And like the Godly men and women of old; we find the secret to living a victorious Christian life. Our trials through life teach us the value of our life in Christ. Through our changes, challenges, faults and failures, and also in good times and victories; we must always remember that God is the one who sets the standard for the people who are called by His name. And nothing in His vast universe could ever change that. David's victories would not come easily. He would be continually reminded of his past, but this is where he must wrestle with God in the strength which He provides. With persistence he disciplines himself as God gives him continued strength to overcome in life.

The ability of self-discipline is one of the highest standards and greatest virtues of Christian living. To access this discipline may not always seem easy to do. In those times when it looks like God has changed His mind about the things He has declared over our lives; we don't turn and run in the opposite direction. But we arise in the grace which He has provided for us, and by the faith which He has supplied to us; we make a demand on His provisions for us. And His promise is…

"But my God shall supply all your need according to his riches in glory by Christ Jesus." Philippians 4:19 (KJV)

God's promises to His people are sure, and His words are true. Everyone who is called by His name will ultimately prevail. One way or another, He will empower us to overcome and immerge into our purpose in life, even if that means we have to wrestle with God.

Spiritual Boot Camp

Boot Camp, what do you think of when you hear that? I think of rigorous training, and preparation for some task or event.

The term boot camp is applied to different venues where there are groups of people training, outdoors and in the fitness industry.

The U.S. Army has boot camp sites positioned in different locations throughout the United States. Drill sergeants are usually the instructors responsible for most of what takes place in basic training. They accompany recruits throughout the training process with ten weeks of intense and well-rounded preparation for all elements of service. Instructing and correcting them in everything from firing weapons to the correct way to address a superior and are also largely responsible for the safety of recruits. Boot Camp is only for those who are serious about the transformation process, the process of becoming. Boot Camp was not created to kill soldiers, but to transform them into the best that they can be. Thus, to come through boot camp successfully one must live a particular lifestyle, get sufficient rest, and stay on the proper diet, because literally every fiber of one's being will be pushed to the limit. It is designed that you may go in as a boy, but you'll come out as a man. They go in in one condition, but they come out in a better one.

Training in spiritual boot camp is not so different than the natural, but the rules of engagement and the requirements are for much higher stakes. The training you get in the Army boot camp will help you to get an earthly victory, but spiritual boot camp training has further reaching implications. It prepares us to win battles that take spiritual territory; victories which will eventually place us right in the presence of Almighty God for eternity.

Not everyone who joins the Army survives boot camp. But those who survive it have the assurance of "No Man Left Behind".

God has designed His Boot camp so that everyone entering can get through it, although some fail to realize it.

We have this guarantee from our Heavenly Father and the armies of Heaven; "No soul forsaken".

Hear is a secret that great numbers of people fail to discover while in training. That is, the trainer is not their enemy; learn to co-operate with him. As believers we must learn to trust that the trainer knows what it takes to prepare us for the battles ahead. God has designed our battles in such a way that our victory comes with them.

Sometimes when God is at work strengthening our faith, the way He does it may not be to our liking; but we learn to co-operate with Him and trust that He knows what He is doing. He will get us through it, and we will get the victory! Perseverance in training assures perseverance in battles. We cannot experience on the battlefield what we have not experienced in training. Training is a must if we would triumph, and without it we are not qualified for the fight.

We have to prepare in order to wage spiritual warfare. There are no quick fixes! Our training at times may be more rigorous than the actual battlefield event. It can get to be pretty rigorous.

"Let us not become weary in doing good, for at the proper time we will reap a harvest if we do not give up." Galatians 6:9 (KJV)

We can be confident that successfully coming through boot camp is just what we need to get us through the tough times ahead. The rigorous training of Boot Camp builds our endurance and creates stamina for the battlefield. God's Word is our training guide.

The depth of our endurance in training will determine the height of our victory in battle. We cannot afford to faint in the battle.

"If you faint in the day of adversity, your strength is small." Proverbs 24:10 (KJV)

Those who quit in the bitterness of training are the same ones who never get to taste the sweetness of victory from the battle. We are over comers in Christ; the victory belongs to us! It is ours! Why? Because our training is aimed at, poised toward, and points to our victory. Training is preparation for the greater, not the lesser.

In God's training camp, the more bitter the cup, the sweeter the victory.

"They that sow in tears shall reap in Joy." Psalm 126:5 (KJV)

At times in training, we may feel stressed, but that comes along with the Boot Camp experience as Jesus takes us through the stress of development.

Another key to successfully come through boot camp, is to learn to tap into the Joy of training (accept it and get the most out of it). Well, can you see any other way that we're going to be happy during this ordeal? Focusing on the prize, the reward, and future victory while in process is what keeps us on track. Knowing that with God the benefits will far outweigh any momentary struggle we ever had.

Like men on a road construction site, the signs are set up to allow the men to get their work done, while guiding the traffic past them. The signs are a shield to them.

Psalm 3:3 says: "But you Oh Lord are a shield for me, my Glory and the lifter up of my head."

We can rest in Jesus and be content because He is our shield of protection. We must learn to enjoy the journey, being thankful as the

Lord prepares us during these hours of boot camp without complaining as not to grieve the Holy Spirit. To grieve one is to hurt the heart.

At one time or another, we all have hurt our Heavenly Fathers heart.

But I believe it would hurt Him worse when He has invested so much in us, if we failed to complete our training, aborting it mid-course. Allowing Jesus to complete what He has started within us will enable us to finish our course.

"Being confident of this very thing, that he which hath begun a good work in you will perform it until the day of Jesus Christ." Philippians 1:6 (KJV)

It's Your Move

As the body of Christ, our everyday lives are spent in preparation for our life in eternity. We just spoke about getting through spiritual boot camp. Boot Camp, like all other parts of this life, is in constant change, nothing on the earth is designed to last forever. And so, life is all about changes. Changes mean that there comes a time when we must put into action what we have learned. Boot Camp is over and the battle is at hand. Now that we are on the battlefield, we don't just stand around looking at each other, but we get busy implementing what we have learned and put it into action. Words are not enough. It's time to do… something. It's your move!

I'm reminded of the checkers game that I used to watch my father play when I was a child. The game started with two opponents. Each player begins the game with 12 pieces, or checkers, placed in the three rows closest to him or her. The object of the game is to capture all of your opponent's checkers or position your pieces so that your opponent has no available moves. Basic movement is to move a checker one space diagonally forward. Finally, your action and even your inaction will cost you in some way. In a word, you had to make a decision; you had to make a move!

Jesus alone purchased our salvation; we had nothing to do with it. It was freely given to us. And now we have been brought to a right standing before the Lord. But a right standing without some daily maintenance can be tragic. We are required to maintain and hold dear to us this life of salvation so freely given. If we would remain in right standing before the Lord, we must spring into action and keep praying and sharing God's love with others.

I'm sure there have been times in your life when you were praying and asking the Lord for some particular thing, but there is no apparent answer. And eventually you slipped into that "I'm waiting on the Lord" mode. The Bible does tell us to "Wait on the Lord". But after recounting some of my own life experiences, I find that more often than not, in life experiences; God is waiting on us. In our dilemma while we say we are waiting for God to move, could He be saying to us it's your move?

When things are not happening the way, we expected them to, it is easy to come to conclusions that are not necessarily God's answer for us. We all get impatient at times while waiting for the Lord to act on our behalf. God has an awesome plan for each of us, and ultimately He is in control, but now and then He is saying to you and I, it's your move! Something that is easy to accomplish is not necessarily proof that it has God's approval. Sometimes what we are asking the Lord for may only happen at the cost of something to us.

But at midnight Paul and Silas were praying and singing hymns to God, and the prisoners were listening to them. 26 Suddenly there was a great earthquake, so that the foundations of the prison were shaken; and immediately all the doors were opened and everyone's chains were loosed. 27 And the keeper of the prison, awaking from sleep and seeing the prison doors open, supposing the prisoners had fled, drew his sword and was about to kill himself. But Paul called with a loud voice, saying, "Do your self no harm, for we are all here." Acts 16:25-34 (NKJV)

Paul the Apostle was a man who dedicated his life service to Jesus Christ. This was after he had persecuted the people of God in many of the surrounding towns *(Acts 9:1)*. But when he met Jesus the Savior on the road to Damascus *(Acts 9:5)* he was changed forever. He chose to follow Jesus, but I'm sure he had no plans of ending up in jail for his commitment to Christ. He and Silas were thrown into prison because of their testimony for Jesus Christ. What a challenging dilemma this was. For doing Good they were repaid with evil. And there they were, locked away from the outside world, and from the freedoms they had always known. They could have sat within the prison walls moaning and groaning, complaining and winning, saying woe is me; I'm waiting on the Lord.

Waiting on the Lord! The waiting is only half of the story. How they waited is the other half. How we wait on the Lord is as crucial as that we wait. At midnight they sang hymns of praise to God. Paul and Silas made the exceptional choice to encourage themselves by praising God. The scripture tells us that while Paul and Silas sang, the other prisoners were listening to them. I'm sure the prisoners were amazed at such surprising behavior. Paul and Silas knew that eventually the Lord would answer their prayers. But for this moment it was their move. They did what should come natural for the servants of the Lord.

When life has thrown to us a curve ball that has gotten us off balance, the equalizer is worship. These men had something that the other prisoners didn't have. They possessed a faith and provocative worship which invited the Holy Spirit to intervene on their behalf to God. And God responded to their faith. They realized that it was their move.

As we learn to recognize the times when it's our move, the Lord does great things in accomplishing His will in us. The Lord delivered Paul and Silas from their dungeon of despair, and He will deliver us as well when we realize it's our move. The believer who can worship during hardships comes nothing short of triumph at the end. Learning to maintain a positive attitude about our suffering makes all the difference in the world. If you are ready to arise from the ashes of your despair and to lay hold on new victories in Christ; this is your day, and nothing can hinder you from being victorious in Christ. *It's Your Move!*

The Shifting of a Sphere
(Prophetic and Inspirational)

"Behold, I show you a mystery; we shall not all sleep, but we shall all be changed, In a moment, in the twinkling of an eye, at the last trump: for the trumpet shall sound, and the dead shall be raised incorruptible, and we shall be changed." 1 Corinthians 15:51-52 (KJV)

This scripture scores one of the single most significant events of all time. It describes to us what is known as the Rapture. It will be a sudden, unforeseen and uncalculated interruption into time, which will end an era, and begin another when Jesus returns to take His bride away. It will be a shift that changes everything. Biblical and world history is filled with times and events where God interrupted the normal flow of things by divine providence to fill a mandate according to His perfect will. I believe that we are living in such a time. There is a shift taking place.

In the natural, a sphere is defined as follows:

(Grk) sphaira, "globe, ball" is a perfectly round geometrical object in three-dimensional space that is the surface of a completely round ball.

The center being the point from which the outer parameters extend, all dimensions are subject to the center. Note: (They extend from).

Now imagine the center expanding. If the center shifts, the outer parameters have no choice but to shift with it.

I believe that God is doing a shifting of spheres in the Spirit realm in these days as He sends forth reinforcement to His bride, The Church.

In my lifetime, I have seen how God has set mandates for change. This shifting enables needed changes to take place. There is a great gathering of souls taking place, and the body of Christ is on the edge of the shift. Our lives as Christians have no alternative but to shift as the Lord does this because He is at the center of our lives. This shift jolts whatever is not anchored and shakes off whatever the Lord rejects in our lives. The weights that we have carried and the things that we have been comfortable with will not bring us satisfaction anymore because we have overcome them.

I John 4:4 says: "Ye are of God, little children, and have overcome them: because greater is he that is in you, than he that is in the world."

Because He is the center of our focus, everything pertaining to our lives must respond according to His will for us. There is a shift taking place around the world. Whole nations are being shaken. At the present, refugees have crossed over into almost every other country of the civilized world. It looks like "The times of the Gentiles" spoken of in *Luke 21:24* is coming nearer to a close.

What do you see in the refugee crisis? I know people have different views on this subject. Even some Christians are at odds about it.

In all the commotion I can see the threat of our enemies as they try to secretly infiltrate our Country. But at the same time, I can also see great opportunities for thousands and maybe even millions of people from other Nations have their first opportunity to come to know Jesus Christ. They may otherwise never have this chance. Before jumping to a quick conclusion, this is something for us to sincerely pray about. God may want to receive a harvest out of the refugees. Ultimately, whether we witness to a foreigner or someone from the United States, this is the goal and mission of the Church; Evangelism. There is no shortage of people needing salvation. My prayer is that we may be open, alert, and ready to share God's love with them. The next opportunity to share God's love is shifting in your and my direction.

As gears are shifted in an automobile, each gear progressing to a higher level of speed, so The Spirit of God will cause us to excel in this season. Obedience and a sincere heart will be the gear of shifting.

"If ye be willing and obedient, ye shall eat the good of the land." Isaiah
1:19a (KJV)

Chapter 7

Decisions at the Crossroads of Life

"Enter ye in at the strait gate: for wide is the gate, and broad is the way, that leadeth to destruction, and many there be which go in thereat: Because strait is the gate, and narrow is the way, which leadeth unto life, and few there be that find it." Matthew 7:13-14 (KJV)

At crossroads is where decisions are made. From the outset of time decisions have been at the forefront of life for mankind. From the fall of man in The Garden of Eden unto the present we have heard of multitudes of people in the valley of decision. Making right choices in life is of the utmost necessity.

Adam & Eve's first requirement from God was to choose to obey, but sadly they ultimately failed. Later on in history, their descendants would have this same choice. When Moses speaks to Israel saying *"Choose you this day whom you will serve" Deuteronomy 30:19,* he was telling them that The Lord God Jehovah was their source.

When Abram obeyed God made a covenant with him. He was circumcised as a sign of the covenant. His commitment was such that out of obedience along with his son Isaac, he circumcised himself.

In Ezekiel chapter 37 the Prophet is obedient to the Lord when commanded to prophecy. The Prophet Elijah spoke to Israel saying to them *"don't waste any more time oscillating between two opinions, Choose God or Baal, choose life or Death!* I Kings 18:21 (paraphrase). These are just a few examples of people making decisions.

Because life is filled with choices, decision making is at every intersection. Our decisions will either help or hinder us in route to our destiny. We must stay alert, always being mindful that as followers of Christ our decisions can stir up spiritual warfare.

Since the fall of mankind in the Garden of Eden, through the weakness of his flesh Satan our enemy stirs up trouble for us. His aim is to work against us through our weaknesses to defeat us. We know that he is the enemy of our souls, and more often than not, the tools he uses are within us *(our flesh)*. When we are aware of this fact, we are now available candidates through God's Word to win many great victories. At the point of our greatest weakness is at the point of the enemy's greatest threat. The Apostle Paul had found the key to successful Christian living when he said *...in my weakness, then am I made strong...(I Cor. 12:9-11)*. It was then that the power of God rested on him.

The Bible says that victory belongs to the believer, so we can rejoice and enjoy every victory as Jesus enables us to overcome our weaknesses. He declares to us that we are overcomers in Him.

Along with knowing this we must take security measures. We cannot afford to be so excited with our victories that we let down our guard. Life is a series of battles, and our challenges can sometimes cause setbacks. In those times it is good to know that we are equipped for recovery, and designed to ultimately be victorious in Christ.

In the book of Joshua chapter 5, when Joshua had led the new generation of Israelites to the border of the promise land, each male among them were to be circumcised (verses 5-8) as a commitment to renewing the Covenant formerly made by Jehovah with Abraham. The place where they were circumcised was named Gilgal. It was situated in the east border of the plains of Jericho where the Israelites first encamped after crossing the Jordan River. Here they kept their first Passover in the land of Canaan (5:10). The word Gilgal means *"rolled away the reproach"*. The reproach of their Egyptian slavery was now gone. They were now a new breed of warriors. As they crossed the Jordan River the priests took up twelve stones and they set them up as a memorial. It was the place of remembrance and renewal. These two acts; the choices of remembrance and renewal have been proven throughout the ages to guarantee God's favor on a people. There is always a place in our lives for remembrance and renewal.

God had initiated the terms of the covenant with Abraham, but He held Abraham accountable to cut away his own flesh. Abraham was so convinced of God's promise to him, that in obedience he proceeded to circumcise himself in compliance to the terms of the Covenant. Our circumcision is that of the heart. As with Abraham, we are given the responsibility to do the circumcision part ourselves.

For us in the 21st Century Church, the circumcision signifies that we must separate ourselves from fleshly habits and worldliness. And from sinful habits, behaviors and conduct, that of departing from our old ways, *"mortifying the deeds of the body"* as The Apostle Paul puts it – Romans 8:13 (KJV).

Here is the battle strategy that assures your and my victory. It is the willingness to become circumcised in heart. This is what marks out our success, brands us as the victor; and inscribes favored upon our lives! Thus, we have been called to be a new breed of warriors, a different generation of believers, a conquering battalion, a wreck the house crew as it were. These are the Lord's troops whose preparations are not from this earth, but they are issued from the Heavens.

Upon your decision and mine we will experience these victories when we decide to live our lives God's way. No one is born into this world with the option to avoid making choices. Everyday of life brings us to cross-roads of decision. With every experience a decision is always made. In fact, indecision is a decision. With each new day we learn how to be successful and enjoy this life through a continual succession of choices. We are victorious in Jesus upon our choice to receive Him.

We live peaceably with all men (as much as lieth within us) through the strength which God supplies, but we have to choose to do so.

We have an inheritance in Heaven, which doesn't fade away (I peter 1:4), and we choose to believe it because Jesus said so.

God's instructions to the Nation of Israel were sufficient for them to reach their highest good, to experience life in abundance; and to have the fullest degree of peace that could be expected in life upon entering the Promised Land.

Jesus has set before you and I the options to choose good or evil, and life or death; while assuring us that this life can only be full when we live according to His plans for us.

"For I know the plans I have for you, declares the Lord, plans to prosper you and not to harm you, plans to give you hope and a future." (Jer. 29:11)

Life doesn't always bring to us what we think we want, or when we want it; but we are blessed beyond measure because of all that Jesus has done for us. If we would accomplish greater victories, higher levels of service; and if we would experience broader places of grace, we can only do it by the decision to do what is right in the eyes of The Lord.

"According as his divine power hath given unto us all things that pertain unto life and godliness, through the knowledge of him that hath called us to glory and virtue." II Peter 1:3 (KJV)

When you find yourself at a crossroads in life and you must make a choice, remember that making a good choice is not enough if it is not the right one. Choosing to follow Jesus' lead is always the right choice.

Return To The Place Of Antioch

According to above scriptures, the Christian community at Antioch began when Christians who were scattered from Jerusalem because of persecution fled to Antioch. It was a main point of interest, because it was connected with the progress of Christianity among the non-Jewish believers.

According to the Jewish Historian Josephus, thousands of pilgrims came to Jerusalem for festivals. People came from Africa and Egypt in the south, from Mesopotamia in the east, and from Anatolia and Syria in the north including Antioch on the Orontes River.

Antioch, an important intersecting point for a number of roads, was about 300 miles northeast of Jerusalem in Syria. Antioch was a strategic place and point physically, but it is also spiritually strategic for us.

The famous Jerusalem council held there *(Acts 15:22-33)* is the place where the Apostles and prophets finally got it right and resolved the issue whether the Lord had opened the way for the Gentiles to be saved.

From the council given in the place, the Good news of Jesus Christ went forth into all the world.

Spiritually speaking, you and I have come through the place of Antioch- the place where the Lord first showed us the right way and we began to walk in it. It is the place where Christ's followers were first called Christians *(Acts 11:26)*. With its many roads splitting off into multiple directions, it speaks to us in a spiritual sense of the place that connects to the world for Christ; touching people of all Nations. It also signifies the place of oneness, where they prayed with one heart and one mind, and the Lord responded; He answered them.

The 21ˢᵗ Century Church can learn so much from the situation at Antioch. It needs to stop and do an about face, and return to tread the streets as it were of Antioch once again. There is where the fellowship of the believer is to be found; and where we experienced the quickening power of the Lord Jesus, who is the Day Spring from on high; as spoken of by the Prophet Zacharias the priest *(Luke 1:78)*. Oh, to experience the visitation of the Savior's presence among us like He has done in times past; the place of communion with God, where He loosed the shackles of those who were bound, and where the oppressed was set free.

It all begins with the decision and commitment of the individual.

You see, the place of Antioch serves for us as the place of reckoning, of decision making, of taking our rightful place as a child of God and disciple of Jesus Christ. So shake up your world, do the unthinkable (as far as the world is concerned) go back to Church, get back to fasting and prayer, pick up and read your Bible again, testify to the world about Jesus and may the fire on my altar never burn out as with the Old Testament Levite priests in doing their daily duties in the Temple of God.

The order of the priests was that as each one performed their Temple service consecutively; part of their duty was to keep a perpetual fire going in the Temple *Leviticus 6:12-13 says:*

"The fire on the altar must be kept burning; it must not go out. Every morning the priest is to add firewood and arrange the burnt offering on the fire and burn the fat of the fellowship offerings on it. The fire shall ever be burning upon the altar; it shall never go out."

It is time for us to arise and unite our voices with the voices that still echo from the altars of Antioch, and with truly repentant hearts; return in fellowship before God. This is your and my God-given privilege.

The Blessedness of Discipleship

"And Jesus, walking by the sea of Galilee, saw two brethren, Simon called Peter, and Andrew his brother, casting a net into the sea: for they were fishers. And he saith unto them, Follow me, and I will make you fishers of men. And they straightway left their nets, and followed him." Matthew 4:18-22 (KJV)

In the above scripture Jesus calls the first of His disciples. He was ready to pour of Himself into their lives so that they would do the same for others.

In this chapter I want to aim at making you aware of what Christ has invested in every believer, and that discipleship is not an option after we have come to know Jesus as our Lord and Savior. Making new converts (disciples) is the mission of the Church.

The highest calling in life is to obey the divine directive of going to all nations and making disciples, this is the mission of the Church… according to *(Matthew 28:19-20)*. What is a Disciple? The word disciple refers to a student or an apprentice, who follows the teachings and examples of their Leader, thus; a disciplined student. Discipline comes from the Latin 'discipulus', the source of the word disciple.

Jesus called Simon and his brother Andrew to become His disciples. What does it mean to be a disciple of Christ? Christian discipleship starts with Jesus Christ. He sets the standard. His idea of discipleship is not as much about doing as it is about being, which is an expression of who He is. Everything He did was related to whom He is, which is what He seeks to reveal to the world through you and I; as He makes us more like Him.

Jesus' goal was to develop in His disciples Christ likeness, His character and His ways. He was not interested only in skill oriented followers; no. His aim was getting them to take on His image. He was aware that skills are plentiful; but true discipleship is priceless, because it is more about being than about doing. Discipleship begins with the one who is being the disciplined one. If our lives are going to impact the lives of others for good, we must be sure that our life is worth duplicating. And it can only be worth duplicating if Christ is at the center of it!

We have all been called to disciple others, and we do it in different ways through different methods. The goal is not to forever be the disciple, but to become one who makes other disciples. Disciples for Christ are (as it were) privates being trained for the position of Generals. Mentoring, reconciliation, and evangelism are all akin to discipleship. Effective discipleship begins with knowing who we are in Christ, because His knowledge is the power which enables us to determine what we do for Him. Jesus was well aware of His identity as the Son of God, and that made His every decision clear.

No one trains for a football team just to sit on the sideline; they eventually get into the game. No one signs up for the baseball team only to relax in the dugout. Nor does a soldier set up house in the fox hole on the battlefield. The fox holes are meant to shelter the troops for a time until the right moment to attack the enemy. So, it must be with disciples. After they have received instructions, they move on to become the one who disciples others. This is how the Church grows, this is how the Kingdom of God grows in the hearts of God's people, and this is how His Kingdom comes on the earth as it is in heaven. The body of Christ will rise to its pinnacle when we learn that discipleship is the key to Church growth. When we are busy making disciples for Christ, we come to the realization that at those times when we have said we are waiting for the Lord; we begin to see that actually He is waiting for us. To be a disciple for Christ means that we are representatives and ambassadors for Him.

"We are therefore Christ's ambassadors, as though God were making his appeal through us. We implore you on Christ's behalf: Be reconciled to God."
II Corinthians 5:20 (KJV)

"For we are laborers together with God: ye are God's husbandry, ye are God's building." I Corinthians 3:9 (KJV)

Jesus is calling people just like you and me to join with Him in the greatest and most significant endeavor we could ever be involved in. That is, the establishment of His eternal Kingdom through the winning, building up, and sending forth of disciples to the world for Christ.

And that people of all nations may have the opportunity to hear and receive His Invitation to come and be born again into the eternal family of God! Disciples for Christ are aware that lip service alone doesn't count for much, but love in action is what pleases God. Disciples are co-laborers with God for Christ's sake, and they have the heart of their Savior. We love what He loves, and shuns whatever He disregards. The disciple's highest goal in life is to please his Master in all things. Disciples for Christ make an impact on their world for good through the service of selfless love, because the Law of God is in their hearts.

"Do not look at his (Eliab) appearance or at the height of his stature, ... for God sees not as man sees, for man looks at the outward appearance, but the LORD looks at the heart." 1 Samuel 16:7 (KJV)

The Great Shepherd

"The Lord is my shepherd; I shall not want. He maketh me to lie down in green pastures: he leadeth me beside the still waters. He restoreth my soul: he leadeth me in the paths of righteousness for his name's sake." Psalm 23:1-3 (KJV).

The combination of shepherd and sheep is pictured throughout Biblical history. In O. T. times, it described God's relationship to His people, and in N. T. times as well, it describes Jesus' relationship with all who will obey and follow Him. The proper order is that Shepherds lead and sheep follow, shepherds instruct and sheep obey.

In the above Psalm David speaks from experience using the analogy of Shepherd and sheep. He had a clear understanding of the relationship between the two. The first five words in the scripture *"The Lord is my Shepherd"* describe the entire narrative. They are the full scope of the Chapter. They encapsulate the objective of the entire 23rd Psalm, thus, the Psalm's main focus is not on the sheep, but on the Shepherd. Although the story tells us at length about the sheep as it focuses on their vulnerabilities and dependence on the Shepherd, everything culminates with the Shepherd's care.

Sheep are loyal creatures and are easily led, they recognize the voice of their Shepherd.

John Chapter 10 gives us a vivid picture of the relationship of the Shepherd and the sheep. John also shows us the contrast between the Shepherd and the thief. In verses 1 and 10 He gives warnings of the presence of the thief, while in *verses 2-9* He describes who the real Shepherd is. Notice the phrase "The Good Shepherd". This lets us know that there can be bad shepherds. Jesus said, *"All that ever came before me are thieves and robbers: but the sheep did not hear them" (verse 8).* Jesus is The Great Shepherd, and we are the sheep. The Shepherd's concern for the sheep is expressed in His care for them: The Great Shepherd (Jesus) loves the sheep so that He has raised under shepherds to gather, nourish and to care of His flock until the great day when He will gather them receiving the harvest of the souls which His has planned. Jesus has shown His love and care for the sheep by giving them under shepherds who have the heart of the Great Shepherd.

God spoke of David as being a man after His own heart:

"And when he had removed him (King Saul), he raised up unto them David to be their king; to whom also he gave testimony, and said, I have found David the son of Jesse, a man after mine own heart, which shall fulfill all my will." Acts 13:22 (NKJV)

After God removed King Saul, He replaced him with King David whose heart was right with God.

In another place in the Nation of Israel's history the Lord spoke to the Prophet Jeremiah, (3:15) saying…

And I will give you pastors according to mine heart, which shall feed you with knowledge and understanding. And in New Testament times the same message came to the Apostle Peter, (I Peter 5:2-4) concerning the under shepherds, or Pastors. It reads…

"Feed the flock of God which is among you, taking the oversight thereof, not by constraint, but willingly; not for filthy lucre, but of a ready mind; Neither as being lords over God's heritage, but being examples to the flock. And when the chief Shepherd shall appear, ye shall receive a crown of glory that fadeth not away."

Only when the under shepherd's heart is pure can the sheep know the heart of The Great Shepherd.

You see; the whole idea behind the Shepherd and sheep relationship is that the sheep will know the shepherd's care of them as He brings them into the right place with the Shepherd. Spiritually speaking; into the secret place where they can *"abide under the shadow of The Most High"* as stated in *Psalm 91*.

Jesus is your and my Great Shepherd for this life and for eternity. He stretches out His rod of love and care to correct and to guide us into all truth through the duration of our lifetime upon earth. The Great Shepherd awaits us with the expectation of a progressive relationship with you and me.

Concerning the shepherd's relationship toward their sheep, the top priority and focus is the health of the sheep. The shepherd is always looking for defects or disease among his flock, ready to heal it quickly, to guard against the loss of even one among them. The spreading of disease could cost the shepherd the entire flock of sheep. This is the aim and pursuit of our Great Shepherd; to bring us in from the fields of the cares of this life; and into His fold for eternity.

A Healthy Heart Condition

Jesus is interested in your and my health, both natural and spiritual. In our physical bodies, if the heart is sick then the whole body is sick. As it is with the natural, so it is with the spiritual.

Jeremiah 17:9 *says: The heart is deceitful above all things, and desperately wicked; who can know it?*

If one would make any spiritual progress, if any impact for good on the lives of others, or maintain a firm footing in their Christian walk; matters of the heart must be closely monitored. And doing so is a full time 24/7 job. The heart along with the mind is the seat of one's intellect; it is the place from which we communicate, think, reason and make decisions. It is also the place where our motives and emotions arise from. The heart is linked to the mind by our emotions. Both have to be constantly guarded against corruption. The heart and the mind are the places where most of the spiritual warfare of life takes place. If the enemy could rule our thoughts, he would win our hearts.

Proverbs 4:23 says: *"Above everything else guard your heart, because from it flows the springs of life." (NIV)*

The heart is the central station of the physical body. If it becomes corrupt the whole body is corrupt.

But a healthy heart means a healthy person, in the natural and the spiritual. Eating right and exercising regularly ensures a great degree of good health. Being careful not to put harmful things into our physical bodies is a must, which always works to our advantage.

What more when it comes to the spirit man? Feasting daily on God's Word insures our spiritual health and well-being against the diseases that come from corrupted lifestyles. And it protects us from the sicknesses that sin brings into our lives. In case you didn't know it, reaching out regularly to others and sharing God's love with them is like a preventive medicine against spiritual maladies and deficiencies. The Lord declared to the Children of Israel that in keeping His laws He would see to it that none of the diseases of Egypt would come upon them.

"Wherefore it shall come to pass, if ye hearken to these judgments, and keep, and do them, that the Lord thy God shall keep unto thee the covenant and the mercy which he sware unto thy fathers:"…

"And the LORD will take away from thee all sickness, and will put none of the evil diseases of Egypt, which thou knowest, upon thee; but will lay them upon all them that hate thee." Deuteronomy 7:12,15 (KJV)

Keeping the heart clean takes hard work, but with God's help through The Holy Spirit we will succeed, becoming over comers through strength supplied by Jesus Christ.

Jesus said in Matthew 5:8 *"Blessed are the pure in heart, for they shall see God." (KJV)*

The human heart is a complex creation. It has potential for the good and the evil. Because of evil hearted men destruction comes upon the land. But when men and women commit their ways to God with an obedient heart, Generations of people can be saved. The heart is the instrument through which the Lord carries out His will in the lives of

His people. What emanates from the heart reveals to other people who we really are. According to *Proverbs 23:7 "As a man thinks in his heart, so is he"*. For that reason, we must *"guard our heart with all diligence"* (Proverbs 4:23). Yes, we must guard and protect it from outside forces that would threaten its well-being. But it is an even greater task to guard it against what could arise from within.

Matthew 15:11 says: (Jesus speaks) *"It is not what goes into the mouth that defiles a man; but what comes out of the mouth, this defiles a man."* That's because it comes out of the heart.

Also, Matthew *15:19* tells us: *"For out of the heart come evil thoughts, murder, adultery, sexual immorality, theft, false witness, slander."*

Up to this point I have shared extensively with you the functions of the human heart. It has a capacity for good and for evil. It pumps blood into every part of the human body. And it feels the emotions of happiness and sadness. But the highest duty of the human heart is to gravitate toward God its creator, and to reach out to other people and lead them to Jesus the Savior. The human heart is a reservoir with a world of potential. Its highest worth and good is seen only in fulfilling its God-given purpose, which is to…. *"Love the LORD your God with all your heart, all your soul, and with all your mind. Matthew. 22:27."* (KJV)

Jeremiah 29:13 says it like this: *"You will seek me and find me when you seek me with all your heart."*

The heart that is committed to serving the Lord reaches its highest plateau of existence, and affects for good everything around it, while simultaneously setting the stage for its eternity.

People can tell where our heart is by what we say and by what we do.

Jesus said, *"Where your treasure is, there will your heart be also" (Matthew 6:21).* Simply put, whatever we love is where our heart is found. This verse speaks of the desires in the heart, and what lifestyle and habits you and I have chosen to keep. At the end of this life everything will come down to what was in the heart. For God will judge us according to what was in the heart. This is something that each of us can never deny, because whatever is in our heart, we own it.

When someone is having concerns about their heart they say I have a heart condition. The condition of the heart means the state of it.

What is the condition of your heart? Have you had a checkup lately, a heart checkup? Have you checked on the state/condition of your heart lately? Not only the physical heart, though that is needed each year; but I also mean your spiritual heart as well.

A sick heart performs poorly not getting out of low gear, while a healthy heart cruises in top gear with peak performance.

If the heart is not healthy the whole person is not healthy. But if the heart is healthy then the whole person is healthy. While we have the opportunity let us serve the Lord, doing good and serving others, which is God's command to us. When we do it with all our heart, we know that we have a reward for all that we have done for Jesus Christ. It is time to have a clean bill of health. It is time for us to have a healthy heart condition.

Chapter 8

Keys to Successful Christian Living

"And behold, a certain lawyer stood up and tested Him, saying, "Teacher, what shall I do to inherit eternal life?"

He said to him, "What is written in the law? What is your reading of it?"

So he answered and said, You shall love the Lord your God with all your heart, with all your soul, with all your strength, and with all your mind, and your neighbor as yourself." Luke 10:25-27

I would like to talk to you about being successful, i. e. being a success in your Christian walk.

What is your idea of success, what does it look like to you?

The definition of success is: 1. Outcome, result. 2. The degree or measure of succeeding.

My focus (Keys to successful Christian Living) raises the question, can a person be a Christian and not be a success at life? The answer is yes. Personally, I believe the first step to becoming a success is learning to share the love of Jesus Christ with others, and that if we are not sharing His love, we are not a success at all.

Jesus has given to us the promise of eternal life, and He will never break that promise. But that promise is conditional. That is, if we meet the requirements upon which the promise was made, only then can we expect to have eternal life with Him. The fulfillment of that eternal life comes through our obedience to His Word.

Upon this we are drawn to the contrast between being successful at something and ultimately being a success at life. I can be successful at something that may not contribute to me ultimately being a success. This brings us to another question. What kind of success in life is of greatest importance to me?

"Every way of a man is right in his own eyes: but the LORD pondereth the hearts." Proverbs 21:2 (KJV)

The word "Ponder" in the above scripture means "to consider or examine attentively, to weigh in the mind their chances of success." Hence, daily the Lord examines the hearts and minds of mankind with the expectation of drawing out of them their potential for the kind of success which matters to Him.

Does simply being a Christian mean that I am a success? Does it mean that it's all rapped up, and the deal is sealed because we are in Christ?

I don't think that's so. Surely it doesn't work quite like that. Everyone wants to be successful, it means that we have achieved something; an accomplishment, which gives one a sense of worth and value. Mankind has a tendency to equate the accumulation of things with real success, but I want to talk not about the quantity of life, but the quality of life.

The dictionary definition of *quantity is "The specified or indefinite number or amount of something"*, while *quality means "The degree or excellence of something"*. The Lord expects quality over quantity.

St Mark 8:36 *asks us, "What doth it profit a man, to gain the whole world, and lose his own soul?"*

Also, In Luke 12:15 Jesus was speaking to a crowd of people, and someone in the crowd said to him *"Teacher, tell my brother to divide the inheritance with me."* Jesus replied, *"Take heed, and beware of covetousness: for a man's life consisteth not in the abundance of the things which he possesseth."*

It seems like this individual was there in the crowd to get more stuff or things from Jesus rather than being interested in obtaining eternal life. Judging from Jesus response, it seems that this man was not just trying to get what would rightfully fall to him by way of inheritance, but covetousness was the issue in his heart. Covetousness in defined as *"desiring something wrongfully or inordinately without regard to the rights of others"*. When covetousness dominates the heart people get hurt, friends separate, and relationships are destroyed. But the quality of one's life is defined in its clearest terms through this: *"You shalt love the Lord thy God with all thine heart, and with all your soul, and with all your might"* (Deuteronomy 6:5). Also, St Mark 12:31 goes on to tell us, *"love your neighbor as yourself"*. In this is realized the quality of life.

The quality of your life and mine are achieved through repetition. It has been said that repetition is the mother of learning. I believe that. It is practice, doing a thing over and over to achieve our goal. A continual resorting to the Word of God and daily implementing it will bring us all the success needed in our lives. It is true as well when it comes to our relationships with others.

Instead of the quantity of life, the quality of life is experienced when it becomes all about sharing God's love with other people. Life becomes sweet and takes on a whole new meaning when it is lived from outside of self and sharing the same selfless love which Jesus shared. A relentless effort to share with others the love of Jesus Christ is our highest plateau of service in life. It is no doubt also God's greatest pleasure from us. This is what brings out the greatest quality of a transformed life; a life that is about more than our own interests.

The day when we succeed at living beyond ourselves will be the day when we will experience the best that life on earth has to offer. All too often this is not realized because it is not always easily achieved. But whoever said that life is supposed to be easy.

It would be easy to quit when you have repeatedly failed at something. But don't quit! Just because you have failed at something doesn't make you a failure. Keep trying until you succeed. Someone has said that success is simply failure tuned inside out!

The early N. T. Church became successful as they focused not on themselves but on the needs of others. This was when the Good news of Christ began spreading all over the then known world. Now that's success! We must get beyond the tight quartered parameters that we have imprisoned ourselves in. If our success is centered on our interests only, we can never impact the lives of others for good, thus, never to experience the true quality of life.

But when we learn to break out of our box, lose sight on ourselves, and focus on the needs of others, life will become far better than we could ever have imagined. When we learn to do this, we experience Joy like we never have before. Then sadness will have to pack up and leave our dwelling, and sorrow will have no hangouts around our houses. They will be locked out of our lives, and we alone will possess the keys to successful Christian living.

The Chance of a Lifetime

"Thus saith the Lord, In an acceptable time have I heard thee, and in a day of salvation have I helped thee: and I will preserve thee, and give thee for a covenant of the people, to establish the earth, to cause to inherit the desolate heritages;"...

"Can a woman forget her sucking child, that she should not have compassion on the son of her womb? yea, they may forget, yet will I not forget thee." Isaiah 49:8,15

The above scriptures are reminders to us that God has a set time for events concerning the lives of mankind. And also, that He is faithful to His Word, even when we have not been faithful to Him.

In the last chapter we talked about having a healthy heart. A healthy heart enables one to seize upon opportunities that otherwise one would not be able to handle. God is consistently presenting fresh new opportunities for His people to enter into areas of greater service for Him. This is our moment, and we are given great opportunities to reach out to people all around us. We cannot afford to be mesmerized by what is happening in our world and lose our focus on what is most important in life. We have the chance of a lifetime to impact our generation for good despite our challenges and the evil that is going on around us. We need only to seize the moment of opportunity.

The saying "chance of a lifetime" is defined as - An extremely important and/or fortuitous opportunity, especially one that is not likely to ever present itself again. i.e. *"once in a lifetime"*.

Although the above definition refers to something which happens by chance, I'm referring to something that is planned. That is, the seizing of a moment according to God's plan for our lives.

Isaiah Chapters 48-56 is God's response to the Nation of Israel's despondency. Being at a point of low moral and spiritual standing, Israel needed to hear from Jehovah the Lord their God. In Chapter 49: 1-9 God reminds Israel that they are His servants, and that they will never be forsaken. He was now ready to rescue them.

Many times in life, we all have been in the kind of predicament that the Nation of Israel found itself in.

Today in the twenty first century Church, the Word to us is... *"Jesus Christ is the same yesterday, today and forever."* Hebrews 13:8

And also, *"I am with you, even unto the end of the world."* Matthew 28:20 (KJV)

Israel's dire situation at that time was only a prelude to what the Lord was about to do in the Nation, because He was not through with them yet.

You may be feeling somewhat like Israel, like God has forsaken you. For the people of God this feeling can be a normal part of the Christian life at times.

Through the power of God, Israel's plight had now prepared them for greater experiences in the service of the Lord. He was now ready to change everything in their favor. Verses 8-26 of chapter 49 assures them that Zion will be restored, it's just a matter of time, the Divine timing of God. History has shown to us that God's Divine timing is sometimes revealed in its full strength when all seems lost; or when things seem virtually impossible. This was where the Nation of Israel had come to. But they could not afford not to trust the Lord now, this was their moment; The Chance of a lifetime to see The Lord accomplish His Word in them as He had promised.

Countless individuals in different arenas of life have gotten their start, were able to forge ahead; and became successful because they were given "the chance of a lifetime" right in the middle of challenging times.

If the expectant mother would decide to abort her baby because she is having excruciating pain, she would forfeit (pay the penalty) and miss the chance of a lifetime. She would never experience the wonders and joy of holding her precious child, teaching it the ways of life, sharing with it in good times and bad, and watching it grow into a mature adult.

Each of the above characters I have spoken of have this in common. Challenge! Whatever our life dilemma, we must come to grips with this truth; that "if there is a victory to be won, challenges will be what brings it. Whatever is happening in our lives, we must let trusting in the Lord be at the top of our list of things that we must do. Despite the odds, waiting on The Lord is always the best thing to do. Waiting on Him *develops in us the stamina and fortitude needed as we enter into higher places of service for Christ. You and I have been given a golden opportunity, the chance of a lifetime in our generation to reach countless individuals in sharing the love of Jesus Christ.*

We don't always know what God has in store for us up the road, around the next bend, or at the next crossroads. But taking a chance on Jesus has always proven that God is faithful to do what He has promised. Who knows, depending on the situation, making ourselves willing to trust the Lord at all costs may end up costing us nothing at all. Sometimes while we are asking Him to work things out, He has already worked it out. He alone knows what the future holds.

Sometimes when we have missed the goal we come out with regret because we took the wrong course of action. But, even then, we don't waste precious time looking back and saying I should have, I could have, or I would have. Instead, we who have trusted the Lord can look back on the situation and say I did. In order to do this, we must seize these moments of opportunity without fear when they arise, because we have been given the chance of a lifetime to make a difference while we are passing through this way.

For Love of the Prodigal

"And the son said unto him, Father, I have sinned against heaven, and in thy sight, and am no more worthy to be called thy son.

But the father said to his servants, Bring forth the best robe, and put it on him; and put a ring on his hand, and shoes on his feet:

For this my son was dead, and is alive again; he was lost, and is found. And they began to be merry." Luke 15:21-22, 24

What is the meaning of the Parable of the Prodigal Son? First of all, let us get the definition of Prodigal. It means:

1. Characterized by profuse or wasteful expenditure, Lavish.
2. A reckless spendthrift.

This Parable found in Luke chapter 15 draws us a vivid picture of the whole reason Jesus came to earth. His mission was to bring salvation to sinful men. The story is about a wayward son, but the main character in the parable is not the son, but the forgiving father. Each of the characters in the story can represent people at different stages in life. Let's explore.

As Jesus tells the story He wants His listeners to know that it is not just a little story, but it is a parable describing God's love for His children who have strayed away from Him. And that He will go to great lengths to rescue them and to save them from sin and its devastating effects.

The father had two sons. Many of us were like the younger son who wanted things to go his way, and to live life as he wished. He did not want to be held accountable to anyone, which was a big mistake for him. Accountability can be visualized as a road which leads to a disciplined life. Where there is no discipline, there you will find chaos and all sorts of unbridled sins. But the Bible provides all the instructions we need for living a disciplined life.

"Because the Lord disciplines the one he loves, and he chastens everyone he accepts as his son." Hebrews 12:6

So, it is good for us because accountability helps to shape a disciplined life. The process of learning to be a disciplined person creates safe zones on the path of one's life, especially for the believer.

This young man would learn this lesson, but he would have to learn it the hard way because of his disobedience.

The elder brother in the parable can represent the self-righteous person, kind of like the Pharisees and teachers of the law of that day who had become selfish and self-centered. Read Luke 15:2.

Unlike the theme of the previous two parables of Luke 15 which focused on the sinners conversion, this parable seems to be compared more to the restoration of a believer into fellowship with the Father. In the first two parables, the owner went out seeking for what was lost (Luke 15:1-10), whereas in this story the father waits and watches eagerly for his son's return. But in all three stories is demonstrated God's great love for each of His children. In this story we can see the scripture fulfilled that states… *"the goodness of God leads men to repentance"*. Read Romans Chapter2 verse 4.

But how did all these things come to be? How a young man with such great potential could come to this? And what happened that the younger son wanted his inheritance early? He would have eventually received it through patiently waiting for it. He seems to have had no concept of earning what was to come to him. Plus, he was not very considerate of the hard work his father had put into it. It is amazing that there is no record of the father having an argument with his younger son when the son had asked for his inheritance early. The scripture simply says: *"And he divided unto them his living"*.

Perhaps, at this point Jesus wanted His listeners to know through sharing this parable of an earthly father's willingness to let his son choose his path in life; that they would see our heavenly Father's willingness for us to choose, but to choose what is right. The Holy Spirit is a perfect gentleman, He never violates our will, but He is constantly beckoning and nudging us on to choose and do what is right and pleasing to Him.

Instead of rebuking his son, the father, patiently, and no doubt with a sad heart grants him his request.

The younger son was about to learn the lesson that *"a man's life does not consist in the abundance of his possessions"* (according to Luke 12:15). He would also learn that he could not buy happiness and contentment in life. He was thinking only of himself and what he could get. This was selfishness!

Harboring selfishness in the heart always ends up bringing hurt to others. This young man showed a grave disrespect to his father's love and hard work by asking for his inheritance now.

His father grants him his request and off he goes on a spending thrift, and living for the moment. Apparently, he was not thinking that his inheritance would be exhausted after a while.

Here is a picture which parallels a disobedient child of God who would choose to begin living according to the world's standards. Not a good choice. Repentance is the only good that can come out of their situation. Until they repent, they ultimately can only find defeat in life; and so, it was with this young man.

"And when he had spent all, there arose a famine in that land; and he began to be in want.

And he went and joined himself to a citizen of that country; and he sent him into his fields to feed swine.

And he would fain have filled his belly with the husks that the swine did eat: and no man gave unto him." Luke 15:14-16 (KJV)

Now here he is in a foreign land, his party money runs out, he has nowhere to live, and nothing to eat. So, he finds a job working for a Gentile citizen of that country in order to survive. The results of his frivolity and riotous living was not what he had expected. The memory of his riotous lifestyle only reminded him that he had chosen the wrong path for his life.

Jesus doesn't tell us the young man's nationality in the story, but if he was a Jewish fellow in this situation, he had a double problem at this point. It is understood that the Jews did not eat swine, for that reason they would not normally be around them in any way. It was said to be unclean to them (Leviticus 11:7). Not only were the Jews forbidden to eat any swine flesh, but this young man would also be at risk if he even touched or were touched by the swine while feeding them. The Mosaic Law had forbidden even touching swine (Leviticus 11:8). At the least, he *"would fain"* (was tempted to) *eat the husk that they did eat.* Luke 15:16 (KJV)

Desperation will cause people to do things they would not normally do. We often say what we would not do in life, but if our choices and decisions in life are not wise ones, they can leave us in a desperate situation. Desperation could change the tune of that song for all of us. It is no secret that we all must reap what we sow according *Galatians 6:7*. The same things this young man did not want to do for his father, he had to do for this Gentile here in a foreign land, that is; to lay hold on the responsibilities of life that fell to him.

Everybody knows that suffering is a natural part of human life, but much of our suffering would be avoided if we didn't bring it upon ourselves. Oh, that our choices and decisions in life were right every time. Of course that is wishful thinking, because we are just not perfect.

But a wise and caring father's love doesn't run out when his children are disobedient. Neither does he stop loving them when they mess up. All the while that the son was in disobedience, the love of the father continued with the expectation that the son would see the error of his ways and return.

"And when he came to himself, he said, How many hired servants of my father's have bread enough and to spare, and I perish with hunger!"

At rock bottom it is sometimes the place of our greatest potential. It is the place where our options are narrow and our sense of choice is focused. The place where we recognize and begin to use the life tools that God has made available to us to re-align us with His perfect will.

This young man had finally come to his senses, realizing that although his father had given him the freedom to choose his own way, still his father knew what was best for him. Surely the goodness of God leads men to repentance. Time has a way of bringing us to our senses, and trouble has a way of getting us back into our right place. Thank God that He is greater than our bad choices, and His love stronger than our weaknesses.

Observe the Father's abundant love: It is higher than the highest mountain, deeper than the oceans great and wide; it takes hold of the universe around us, yet He calls to each of His children from deep inside. Awesome!

This young man's will was strong, his plans were big, his fall was hard, his desperation overwhelming, but His father's love was greater than all these. The outside forces that surrounded him could not squelch or smoother out the fire of his father's love on the inside. The father's love had been planted within the heart of his son long before the son chose to step out of his father's care.

This story paints the perfect picture of our Heavenly Father's love for you and me. He loved us and provided for us long before we came on the scene. The love of our God is greater than the sins of sinful men. The love of this father set no boundaries when it came to rescuing his son. The son had found the key to his father's heart, and to his favor. Repentance! Nothing else could have ever brought the son back into fellowship and right standing with his father.

Jesus has gone to great lengths to redeem you and me. He came all the way from Heaven to show us the way. His life was an example for us as to how we should live. He experienced rejection, ridicule and slander for us. He suffered, bleeding and dying on the Cross for wayward and disobedient children who wanted to have it their way. But the waywardness of His sons and daughters could not keep Him away nor diminish His great love for us.

"But God commendeth his love toward us, in that, while we were yet sinners, Christ died for us.

Much more then, being now justified by his blood, we shall be saved from wrath through him." Romans 5:8-9 (KJV)

Repentance always causes our Lord to draw near to us.

The son returns, repents as he said he would while in a foreign land, and is restored to right standing with his father.

We all were prodigals at times in our lives when we had wondered away from our Heavenly Father. We fell into all sorts of sins and found that our way was not the way of our Father. Sin has taken its toll on too many of God's people. Even today He extends His loving hands to us. He restores us that we also might extend a loving hand in His name to others saying...

"Come unto me, all ye that labor and are heavy laden, and I will give you rest.

Take my yoke upon you, and learn of me; for I am meek and lowly in heart: and ye shall find rest unto your souls." Matthew 11:28-29 (KJV)

As the father waited for his prodigal son to return, so Jesus waits not only for those who have wandered away from His Church, but for those who have never known Him to come home.

Maintaining Christian Integrity in a Corrupted World

"The righteous man walks in his integrity; His children are blessed after him." Proverbs 20:7 (KJV)

As Christians, the highest priority in life is the commitment to maintaining our walk with Christ, even when we know that commitment will always be tested.

Jesus paid the ultimate price for our salvation by the shedding of His blood on Calvary's Cross. There was no other sufficient sacrifice, because the giving of His life was the only way to attain our salvation.

And now that God our Father has drawn us to Himself through the Son, we must maintain a right standing in Him to continue His work of bringing others to the Lord, even if that means we have to suffer now and then. We must tell them and show them that He loves them. How will they know if we don't tell them? We are His people, and it is up to us to continue sharing that same love of The Father which He shared.

The dictionary definition of *Maintain* is: "To keep in an existing state: to preserve from failure or decline: to uphold and defend a position. *Integrity* means (1) An unimpaired condition: soundness: (2) firm adherence to a code of moral or artistic values: incorruptibility: (3) "The quality or state of being complete or undivided."

In a fallen world full of sinners who have become so corrupted; it is easy to become mixed in with the trend of the times. There is no shortage of sin or sinners in the world; we can see the effects of it through constant reminders every day. Sometimes we are challenged in today's society to lower our standard and to accept a lesser position than what the Lord requires. But despite the challenges, we can and we must maintain our Christian integrity. Although each day is new to us, challenges and testing are not. Therefore, maintaining the integrity of Christ likeness must be an integral part of our daily Christian walk.

The survival (and might I add) the advancement of any Nation, any community, any Local Church, any family or individual will be determined by their integrity. Integrity is not something that is obtained automatically; neither do we just stumble upon it. It is set before us by God with the expectation that we will make the effort to lay hold of it. And through God's help we achieve it. Yet in acquiring it some resistance is to be expected.

In the book of *Job* chapter 2 verses 9-10, it reads…

"Then his wife said to him, "Do you still hold fast your integrity? Curse God and die!"

I believe that we all would agree that Job's wife spoke out of frustration and grief about his situation. Be that as it may, she was out of control with unwise advice for him. And besides, I think that if he had done such a thing as to curse God; surely that would be the quickest way for him to die.

We are familiar with the book of Job as the first of the Old Testament Prophetical books that deal with the problem of suffering. But if we step back a bit and examine the book more closely, we will see it in a clearer light, and get the bigger picture; that is, the reason behind Job's suffering. The aim in the story of Job is to show us that in the midst of suffering God deals directly with mankind and creates within him God's kind of integrity.

The lesson that we take away from Job's plight is that in the worst of times a person can maintain their God given gift of integrity.

So, the Lord, through Job's dilemma, works to develop within him a new level of integrity.

In chapter 27 of the book Job seems to show a bit of piety, as he defends his integrity against his three friends. But the most important thing to know concerning Job's plight was not whether he was right in the eyes of his friends, but rather, the question needed to be answered; had he allowed the Lord to bring his integrity to the surface. Whatever integrity he had to defend, it was there only because God had placed it there.

In Job chapter 42 God declares His own integrity to Job by showing Job his frailties and helplessness before the Lord Almighty.

It is easy for us to think that the story is about Job finally proving to his friends that he was righteous. No, that's not it at all! It is about God convincing all the participants present (and the rest of us who were not there) that He alone is the one who raises and maintains men and women of integrity.

In Job Chapter 2, God Himself had spoken of Job's integrity when He asked Satan *"Have you considered my servant Job…. Yet he maintains his integrity,"* (verses 3a, and 3c).

For the purpose of building integrity, God allows Satan to afflict Job; a prosperous and pious Jew with hardships that tested his faith. Out of this great trial, Job's faith would grow stronger. Growing faith creates a platform for integrity of a godly sort.

Through our challenges of life The Lord is shaping you and I into people of integrity. Satan desires to rob us of our integrity. He doesn't like our testimony, and he wants you and I to doubt our journey. Don't let him! When he closes in and attacks you on the right and on the left, in front and from behind, and you want to get out; you must attack him with God's Word. We have God-given authority, so we declare…The Lord rebukes you Satan! The blood of Jesus prevails against you! Jesus calls you the cursed of God! Jesus declares that you are a liar! Jesus declares my victory over you! I belong to God! I cast you out! Get thee behind me Satan in the name of Jesus!

People of integrity are good and wise decision makers. They carefully observe a thing in order to make the right choice. They study and search out a matter before engaging in it. They think before they speak. Here is wisdom: People of integrity are more ready to listen than they are to speak. Even if they already know the answer to a question, they carefully weigh out their words before their words come out. They are not perfect, (without flaw), not even Christians; but they strive for perfection according to God's Word.

In the Prophet Jeremiah's day when the Lord was moving among His people the Israelites to build His integrity into their lives, He gave Jeremiah this Word which sums up the matter of integrity.... *"Let not the wise man glory in his wisdom, Let not the mighty man glory in his might, Nor let the rich man glory in his riches; But let him who glories glory in this, That he understands and knows Me, That I am the Lord, exercising loving kindness; Judgment, and righteousness In the earth. For In these I delight, says the Lord." Jeremiah 9:23-24 (KJV)*

In the New Testament, Paul gives us the recipe for a life of integrity...

"Finally, brethren, whatever is true, whatever is honorable, whatever is right, whatever is pure, whatever is lovely, whatever is of good report, if there is any excellence and if anything worthy of praise, think (dwell) on these." Philippians 4:8 (NKJV)

Living according to God's Holy Word develops His integrity within us.

The First Dominion

"Now it shall come to pass in the latter days that the mountain of the Lord's house shall be established on the top of the mountains, And shall be exalted above the hills; and people shall flow to it."

Many nations shall come and say, "Come, and let us go up to the mountain of the Lord, to the house of the God of Jacob; He will teach us His ways, and we shall walk in His paths." For out of Zion the law shall go forth, and the word of the Lord from Jerusalem." Micah 4:1-2 (KJV)

In this last section I want to aim at reminding you of your heritage as a follower of Jesus Christ, and that suffering for Him is to be viewed as a privilege and not to be dreaded. In the place where we learn to view suffering as favor and not as an imposition is the place where life actually begins. We are citizens of the Royal Kingdom emanating from the Heavens, The greatest of Kingdoms, an eternal and vast Domain. We are part of The Royal family of The King of Kings who rules The First Dominion. Dominion: Means – Sovereignty; control.

Supremacy, dominance, superiority, preeminence, authority, mastery, command and government are synonymous with Sovereignty.

From the beginning of time mankind has made all kinds of efforts and attempts to establish their own kingdom. We want things to go as we wish, and to have a feeling or a since of control. But time has shown to us that it is a dangerous thing for men to be in absolute control of their own destiny. We possess life that we did not give; we breathe air that we did not produce, and we have a soul which we did not create. Since we are not the creator of any of the above, we are held accountable for what we do with this life which has been given to us. Everyone and everything in creation is held accountable to God who made all things.

Somewhere in God's eternity past, Lucifer decided he wanted a kingdom. But almost as soon as he got started his Kingdom was thrown down to the sides of the pit.

"How you are fallen from heaven, O Lucifer, son of the morning! How you are cut down to the ground, You who weakened the nations! For you have said in your heart: I will ascend into heaven, I will exalt my throne above the stars of God; I will also sit on the mount of the congregation on the farthest sides of the north; I will ascend above the heights of the clouds, I will be like the Most High. Yet you shall be brought down to Sheol, To the lowest depths of the Pit." Isaiah 14:12-15 (KJV)

In the first chapter of this book, we shared with you an excerpt from some Hebrew writings of "The book of Enoch" (Ancient Jewish writing). We explained to you the plans of the Fallen Ones (Wicked Angels) who left their first estate according to (Jude 1:6) and how they planned along with Satan, to build their anti-God Kingdom on the earth. We spoke of their corrupt offspring; the result of Angels having sexual relations with women see (Genesis chapter 6). From their offspring is where we get the classification of Demons.

Much of the evil in the world today; the corruption and evil mindedness of men is a result on Demonic influence.

I once watched part of a TV saga called "Game of Thrones".

Its setting is amidst medieval times. It's the depiction of two powerful families; kings and queens, knights and renegades, liars and honest men playing a deadly game for control of the Seven Kingdoms of Westeros, and to sit atop the Iron Throne. They are "vying for the Throne".

Well, the depiction and tones of the saga speak more of reality than many people know. I'm not promoting the saga, but in a real sense it parallels the reality of the wicked attempts of Satan and his followers to break down and overthrow the Kingdom of God.

In our world, the strongholds over Governments and Nations (which are the principalities and powers spoken of in the book of *Ephesians chapter 6)* are trying to govern over and to be the ones who determine the outcome of mankind's existence by their treachery. They want to steal the Kingdom of God from the hearts of men (read Luke 17:20-21). But their diabolical efforts are futile, and they and their actions will be cut off and driven into oblivion by God.

The first four verses of the book of *Micah Chapter 4* describes what will take place in the Millennial Kingdom, when Jesus Christ will set up His rule on earth to renovate it. It says.....

"The house of the Lord shall be established in the top of the mountains, and it shall be exalted above the hills." (Verse 1b)

Jesus Christ will bind Satan for a thousand years according to *(Revelation 20:2)*. The Millennial reign of Jesus Christ is described as being the last great effort of getting men to turn completely from their sinful lifestyles to the living God. Then after His thousand-year reign, Satan will be loosed for his last season of troubling men on earth by deceiving world Nations into war against the Nation of Israel. Then comes the Great war; the war of all wars, Armageddon; at which time Satan is defeated by Jesus Christ with the sword of His mouth, and Satan is done away with forever.

"And when the thousand years are expired, Satan shall be loosed out of his prison,

And shall go out to deceive the nations which are in the four quarters of the earth, Gog and Magog, to gather them together to battle: the number of whom is as the sand of the sea.

And they went up on the breadth of the earth, and compassed the camp of the saints about, and the beloved city: and fire came down from God out of heaven, and devoured them.

And the devil that deceived them was cast into the lake of fire and brimstone, where the beast and the false prophet are, and shall be tormented day and night for ever and ever." Revelation 20:7-10 (KJV)

As out of control as things may appear to be in our world right now, God is in control. His plan and expectation for mankind have never and will never change from His original determination.

Jesus' great sacrifice on the Cross has given us power for victorious living. But in order for us to successfully live out the Christian life here on earth we must be fully convinced of who's in charge. Although the dictates and demands of our daily lives sometimes suggest the opposite of what the Lord declares, God's Word is true, it is immutable (unchanging).

Witnesses to the First Dominion

The Bible records a list of witnesses who were convinced of God's eternal Dominion as they trusted themselves to His care and security.

Doctor Luke:

"We are surrounded with a great cloud of witnesses according to Hebrews Chapter 12 verse 1 which testify to us of God's Omnipotence."

The Apostle Paul:

"And we know that all things are working together for the good of those who love the Lord." Romans 8:28 (KJV)

"So that at the name of Jesus EVERY KNEE WILL BOW, of those who are in heaven and on earth and under the earth...." Philippians 2:10-11 (NASB)

King David :

"The earth is the Lord's and the fullness thereof, the world and they that dwell therein." Psalm 24:1 (KJV)

"King David Israel's second King was convinced of God's eternal Dominion when he declared..."

"For the kingdom is the Lord's: and he is the governor among the nations." Psalm 22:28 (KJV)

Habbakuk:

When the Prophet Habbakuk brought his complaint before the Lord for the injustice done to his Nation, *(Chapter 1 verses 2-4)* he asked the Lord how long He would allow the wicked to prosper and take advantage of the righteous, and not listen to the prayers of His people. Here was God's answer to Him.

"And the Lord answered me, and said, write the vision, and make it plain upon tables, that he may run that readeth it." (Chapter 2 verse 2) "For the earth shall be filled with the knowledge of the glory of the LORD, as the waters cover the sea." Habbakuk 2:14 (KJV).

Baalim:

In the book of Numbers God speaks to Baalim the son of Beor in response to the wicked King Balak's request to curse the Nation of Israel and to devour the righteous. God's answer to him was…

"He hath not beheld iniquity in Jacob, neither hath he seen perverseness in Israel: the LORD his God is with him, and the shout of a king is among them." Numbers 23:21 (KJV).

Isaiah:

The Prophet Isaiah speaks also of Christ's Sovereignty and eternal rule overall, declaring in His Prophecy of the coming Messiah…

"Of the increase of his government and peace there shall be no end, upon the throne of David, and upon his kingdom, to order it, and to establish it with judgment and with justice from henceforth even for ever. The zeal of the LORD of hosts will perform this." Isaiah 9:7 (KJV)

Daniel:

"And he changes the times and the seasons: he removes kings, and sets up kings: he gives wisdom to the wise, and knowledge to them that know understanding:" Daniel 2:21 (KJV).

Daniel 7:14 - "And there was given him dominion, and glory, and a kingdom, that all people, nations, and languages, should serve him: his dominion is an everlasting dominion, which shall not pass away, and his kingdom that which shall not be destroyed." Isaiah 9:4 (AKJV)

Observe this mystery:

Luke 17:20-21 – *"And when he was demanded of the Pharisees, when the kingdom of God should come, he answered them and said, The kingdom of God comes not with observation: Neither shall they say, See here! or, see there! for, behold, the kingdom of God is within you." (AKJV)*

John:

The Apostle John on the Isle of Patmos saw the end of all things coming when Jesus declares to him…

"And there came loud voices in heaven, saying "The kingdoms of this world have become the kingdoms of our Lord and of His Christ. And He will reign forever and ever." Revelation 11:15 (KJV)

Jesus Himself declares: *"I am Alpha' and Omega, the beginning and the end, the first and the last." Revelation 1:8*

After these brief moments, hours, days, weeks, months and years here on earth; time must end and give way that we may enter into the eternal state where time is no more. God has prepared in the Heavens, His Domain; a place for everyone who has lifted up the blood stained banner of Christ throughout the years of our existence. And there is a reward for those who have laid down their lives for Jesus the Christ of God.

To suffer for Christ is to bear a cross which every believer must bear, but not one of His servants will be lost who have trusted in Him.

The world will continue to exist until He decides - It Is Finished!

His Cross has not disintegrated, so there are no splinters of it remaining for all who follow Him. And there are a few leftover nails that each of us as His children will experience in this life. But that is not an indictment, instead, it is the highest honor that can be bestowed upon anyone. We have been invited to the Royal Wedding and have become members of The Royal family of God. He has promised He will be with us to the end and then rapture us into glory. His promises can be trusted, because His Word is forever settled in the Heavens:

"For ever, O Lord, thy word is settled in heaven." Psalm 119:89 (KJV)

God's Kingdom is an everlasting Kingdom. His Dominion covers all that exists. It is the first Kingdom, and it will be the last one. We are His children and we accept His invitation to live in Christ's Kingdom with Him for eternity.

About the Author

Willie Johnson was born on July 23, 1952, in Laurinburg, North Carolina, to John and Lucy Johnson. He is the eight of fifteen children. Willie received Jesus Christ as his Lord and Savior in the summer of 1972 after recovering from a struggle with drugs. Then he became very active in the church, supporting the local ministry. As a psalmist, he played for various groups and choirs.

In 1986, he received the call of God to the ministry and became active in the Church as a deacon and trustee. In 1989, he was ordained as the assistant Pastor at the local Church where he worshiped, and after a few years, he became the Pastor. He served as Pastor/senior Pastor of two churches in New Haven Connecticut, one church in Bessemer City, North Carolina for two years that transitioned to Orlando, Florida for four years.

Currently, he serves as the founder of King's Foundations Ministries, an outreach ministry in Orlando, Florida. He enjoys singing, writing, playing, and recording music. Also writing books. He is also the President of Lord Song music and publishing, and he loves the Lord for giving him the privilege to serve.